The Book of LONDON

The Book of

TAPLINGER PUBLISHING COMPANY
NEW YORK

LONDON

Photographs by
IAIN MACMILLAN

Text by Roger Baker

Published in the United States by
TAPLINGER PUBLISHING CO., INC.
29 East Tenth Street
New York, New York 10003
© 1968 by Michael Joseph Ltd.

All rights reserved. No portion of this book may be reproduced in any form without the written permission of the publisher, except by a reviewer who may wish to quote brief passages in connection with a review for a newspaper or magazine.

SBN 8008-0925-4

Library of Congress Catalog Card Number 69-14436

Printed in Great Britain

Designed by Yvonne Skargon

The photograph on the front endpaper and the photographs of the Stock Exchange demolition and the Kirov Ballet are reproduced by courtesy of the *Sunday Times*

Second Printing

FRONT ENDPAPER
Barrel race on Hampstead Heath: an occasional holiday revival of a traditional country sport

BACK ENDPAPER
The children of Kenley Street, North Kensington

This book began as a list. It was a long, cold, objective list of buildings, streets, some events and many landmarks that, it seemed, added up to London. The sprawling capital was to be recorded simply and unemotionally. A statement of fact: London as it stands today.

A completely objective record of London is, of course, impossible unless the reporter is reduced to the status of an automaton with no thoughts or views of his own. But many of the already available picture books seemed too personal, too idiosyncratic, until London becomes a private world.

Slowly the items were checked off: a bridge, a boat, a statue, a palace. A group of City churches were photographed one cold, blue Sunday afternoon, deserted apart from cats and caretakers and a straggle of sightseers. Two middle-aged women emerged from the narrow streets behind St. Mary-le-Bow into the glassy space of a revised Cheapside. They lamented change, war, rebuilding. Difficult to find one's way about these days. All the old landmarks vanished, remnants merged into new development schemes, modern piazzas and flying pedways of Barbican.

Already the edges of the hard formula were melting slightly, but the search continued. That celebrated study of the curiously oriental profile of Whitehall seen from St. James's Park was recaptured. Take it. Turn around and there's Buckingham Palace, Royal Standard flying, the Queen at home. Take it. Walk down The Mall (look at Admiralty Arch from a traffic island, head on), a sideways glance at Carlton House Terrace, look up at the Duke of York on his column: Pall Mall, Haymarket, New Zealand House, Eros.

Then there were quick train journeys out of central London, flashes of Big Ben between terraced houses, the train carves a straight line between ropes of washing. To Kew, to Hampton Court, to Richmond. Groups of sharply dressed teenagers waiting on Wimbledon Station to go up West for the evening. It's different south of the river; the lights, the fun, the nucleus of all activity is north of the Thames; the south side is domestic, quiet.

And down river by boat (on your left, Traitors' Gate . . .) to Greenwich, to Wren's theatrical river façades flanking Inigo Jones' pretty house built for a Queen. Elderly people sitting in the sun, gazing across the water. Already, sub-consciously, the real book of London was shaping.

The pile of listed photographs grew. They were pictures any visitor to London would like to have taken, and probably would attempt. They were, too, pictures any Londoner would look at and through them see, with a new eye, the backdrop of his existence taken so long for granted. They were an exhaustive record of the stones around us captured with care and imagination. But the attempt to avoid self-conscious impressionism was moving towards a soulless account of fact that in its way was becoming equally meaningless. It was becoming obvious that London should be seen, not with the cold, detached eye of the reporter, but as through the eyes of the people who live and work in it.

The solution was not just a question of suddenly taking photographs of lots of people and pushing them in. It was, rather, realising the intuitive knowledge of when a figure added to the vitality of a scene, when the presence of a person captured an essential quality that was otherwise elusive, when a face alone could replace whole perspectives. Kew Gardens may consist of 288 acres of flowers and plants, but the reality of Kew is reflected in the happy faces of nuns moving through the hot houses. London itself took over, became responsive and the balance was achieved. But the primary object – to present a reasonably inclusive study of London as it stands – has not been obscured; it has, rather, been illuminated.

Presentation of this mass of material was the next problem. Clearly there had to be some coherence and the chosen form should, preferably, add in itself something towards an interpretation of London. Division of the pictures into chronological sections, starting in the morning and ending in the evening, seemed the ideal solution, enabling all aspects of London to be included within each chapter.

So, Carlton House Terrace, originally designed as an exclusive residential row, is seen in its new context as an office block; the splendours of the Royal Opera House are distilled into the monogrammed curtain before which Dame Margot Fonteyn bows; the Royal Hospital in Chelsea is not merely another interesting building, but a place of peace and leisure.

London is continually changing; its skylines are varied with new tower blocks; its old, stately buildings are cleaned and St. Paul's cathedral once more rides high and golden over the City. *The Book of London* captures this essential quality. The famous places are there, many seen as if for the first time, but so are the new ones, the vital symbols of this evolving town.

ROGER BAKER

London Waking

London wakes early. First risers are the porters, buyers and sellers in the major markets: Covent Garden (fruit, vegetables, flowers); Billingsgate (fish); Smithfield (meat); Spitalfields (fruit and vegetables). Later the commuters come crowding in from the suburbs and further. Finally Londoners themselves pack the buses and underground trains. Some rise early for pleasure and river life is never wholly at a standstill

Mist over the river. Early morning at Tower Bridge

Smithfield Market was established in 1614, though the present buildings were completed only in 1869. The great arcades contain more than 15 miles of meat hooks. *Right:* a cart load of meat awaiting local delivery

St. Thomas's Hospital, early morning. Over the river, the Millbank Tower

Morning in Rotten Row, Hyde Park, a sand track for horse riders. The footpaths beside the Row were once fashionable promenades for Sunday morning strollers. Riding in the Row is still a popular pursuit

The start of the London to Brighton Veteran car rally. This annual event was brought to world attention through the comedy film *Genevieve*. The event still attracts a number of remarkably efficient entries

Billingsgate Market. Noted for its fish and its characteristic, vigorous language. The porters' hats are designed to enable them to carry a number of empty crates piled up on their heads.

The Monument, just by Billingsgate market, was built by Sir Christopher Wren and Robert Hooke to commemorate the rebirth of the City of London after the great fire of 1666

Bus queue in Oxford Street

The underground: coming up the escalator at Archway Station

Centre Point: one of the newer tower office blocks; dominates St. Giles Circus, the junction of Tottenham Court Road and Oxford Street

Newspaper seller near the Old Bailey

The Queen's postman, in his brougham, waits for a reply having delivered mail to government offices in King Charles Street between Whitehall and St. James's Park

Left: mail bags and parcel post wait at St. Pancras Station

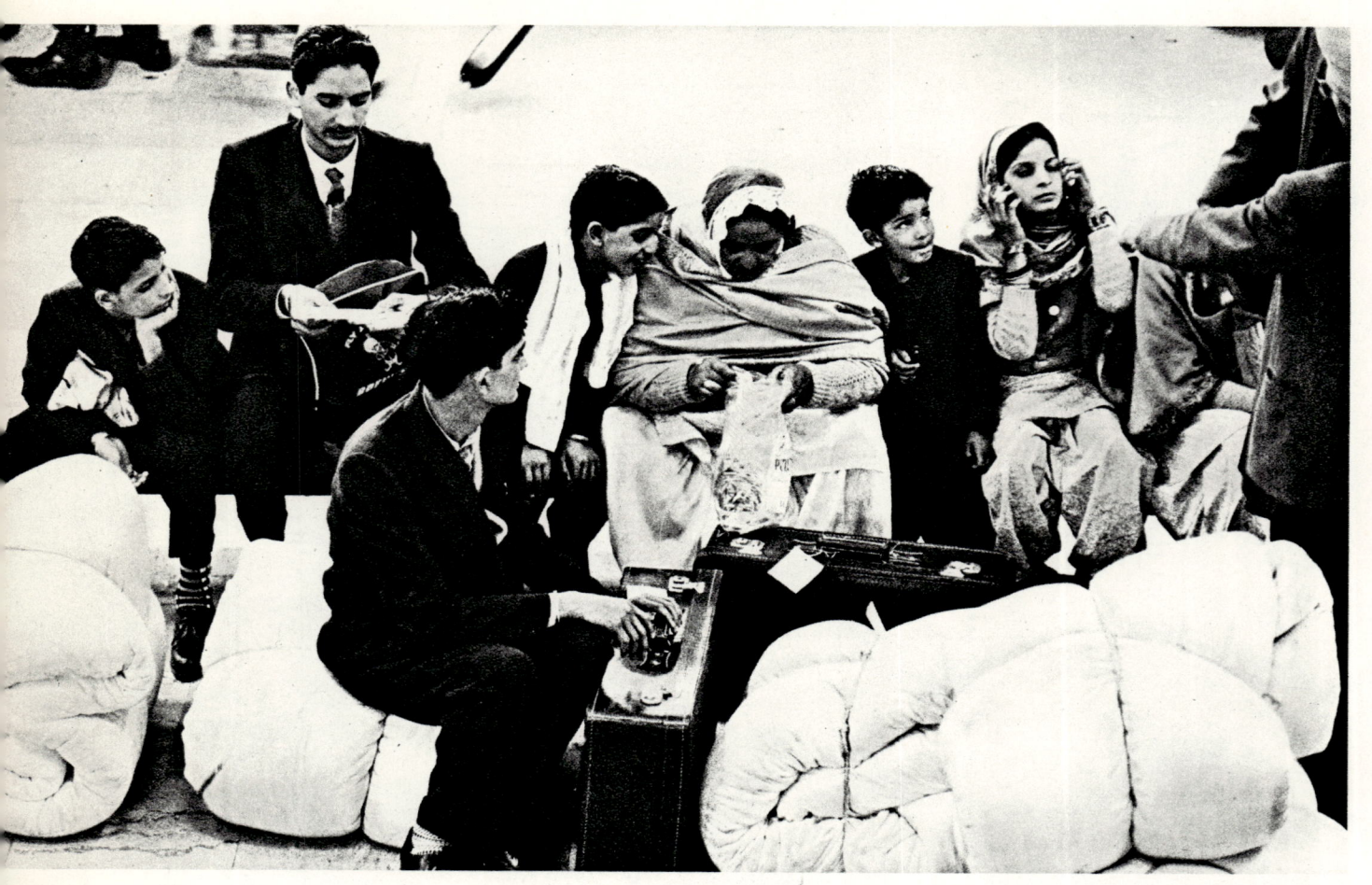

London airport. An Indian family arrive

Right: Waterloo Station, one of the main termini for southern England's home counties and the south coast

Victoria Station

At Victoria Station, an Italian family arrive from a boat train

London Working

London at work. The major centres are the City of London and the City of Westminster. Historically both have always filled their own function, the first as the seat of commerce, the second as the seat of government. Each section of the capital has its own particular working identity: Fleet Street for the press; the Strand for the Law; Soho for music and entertainment; Oxford Street for shopping and the rag trade. Through it all moves the river Thames from the docks, through the Pool of London to its quieter reaches above Battersea

Through morning mist underwriters arrive at Lloyds of London, world authority on shipping, vast insurance concern started in a coffee house in the late 17th century

The Royal Exchange at the hub of the City. No business is conducted there today and the glass-roofed courtyard is used as a museum of Roman and medieval relics. Photograph by courtesy of the Gresham Committee

Wholesale: vegetables sorted for delivery from Covent Garden, central fruit, flower and vegetable market

Retail: flowers for sale on the pavement in Regent Street

34

Mansion House, official residence of the Lord Mayor of London

The Bank of England. Its external wall has no windows. The building within has 10 storeys, three below ground

The Stock Exchange, headquarters of the dealers in negotiable securities. The floor accommodates some 2,500 brokers and jobbers; the first acting as agents for clients, the second as wholesalers in stocks

Right: the building is presently being demolished to make way for new, modern premises

GOODMAN
PRICE G

London Wall. On an area razed by the blitz a vast modern complex of office blocks and residential buildings, also a new theatre

Above: London Wall. 18th century churches and fragments of the Roman wall are retained in the new development

Left: Temple Bar where the Strand ends and the City of London begins; made in 1880

New Scotland Yard, in Whitehall, for many years headquarters of the Metropolitan Police. Their H.Q. has now been moved to a modern block in Victoria, retaining the same name. *Right:* the Royal Courts of Justice, known as the Law Courts, on the Strand

41

Broadcasting House, headquarters of the British Broadcasting Corporation, and the church of All Souls, Langham Place

Somerset House, perhaps the most splendid house in London, built in the mid-18th century. The building now contains government offices, notably the Board of Inland Revenue, the Registry of births, marriages and deaths and the Principal Probate Registry. King's College, one of the incorporated colleges of the University of London is in the east wing

University College, Gower Street. Students sit out under the Corinthian portico. The Slade School of Art is here too

The Royal College of Art in Kensington Gore, built in 1961

Sir Christopher Wren's fine perspective of the Royal Naval College at Greenwich seen from across the Thames. Central is the Queen's House built by Inigo Jones for Anne of Denmark. The National Maritime Museum is housed here

Right: leaf-sweeper in Holland Park, west London

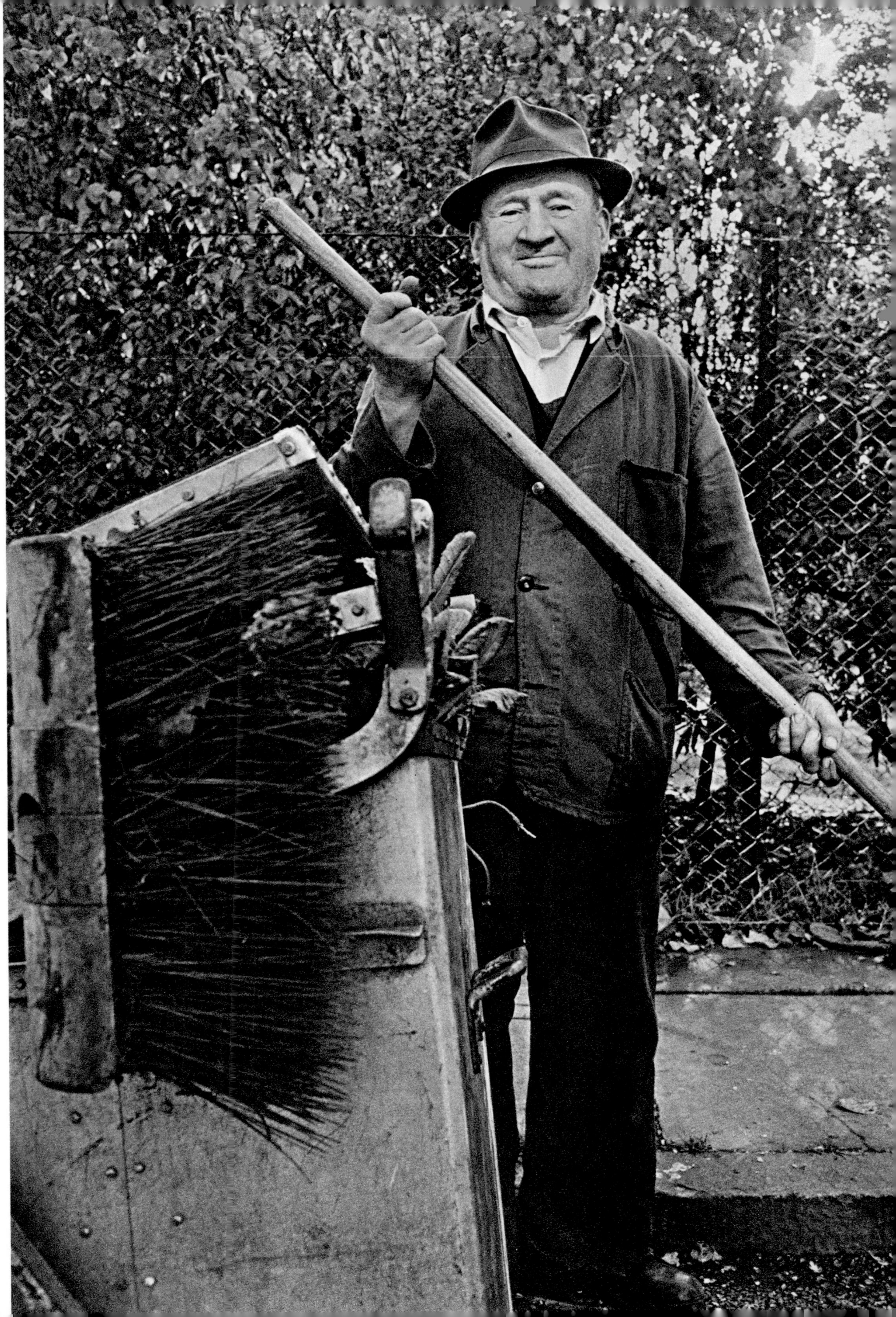

Entrance to the Central Criminal Courts, Old Bailey, built on the site of Newgate Prison. Some of the original stones are used in the building. It is surmounted by a celebrated symbol of the law, a statue of Justice with her scales, seen (*opposite*) reflected in the windows of an office block in Snow Hill. Also reflected, the tower of St. Sepulchre

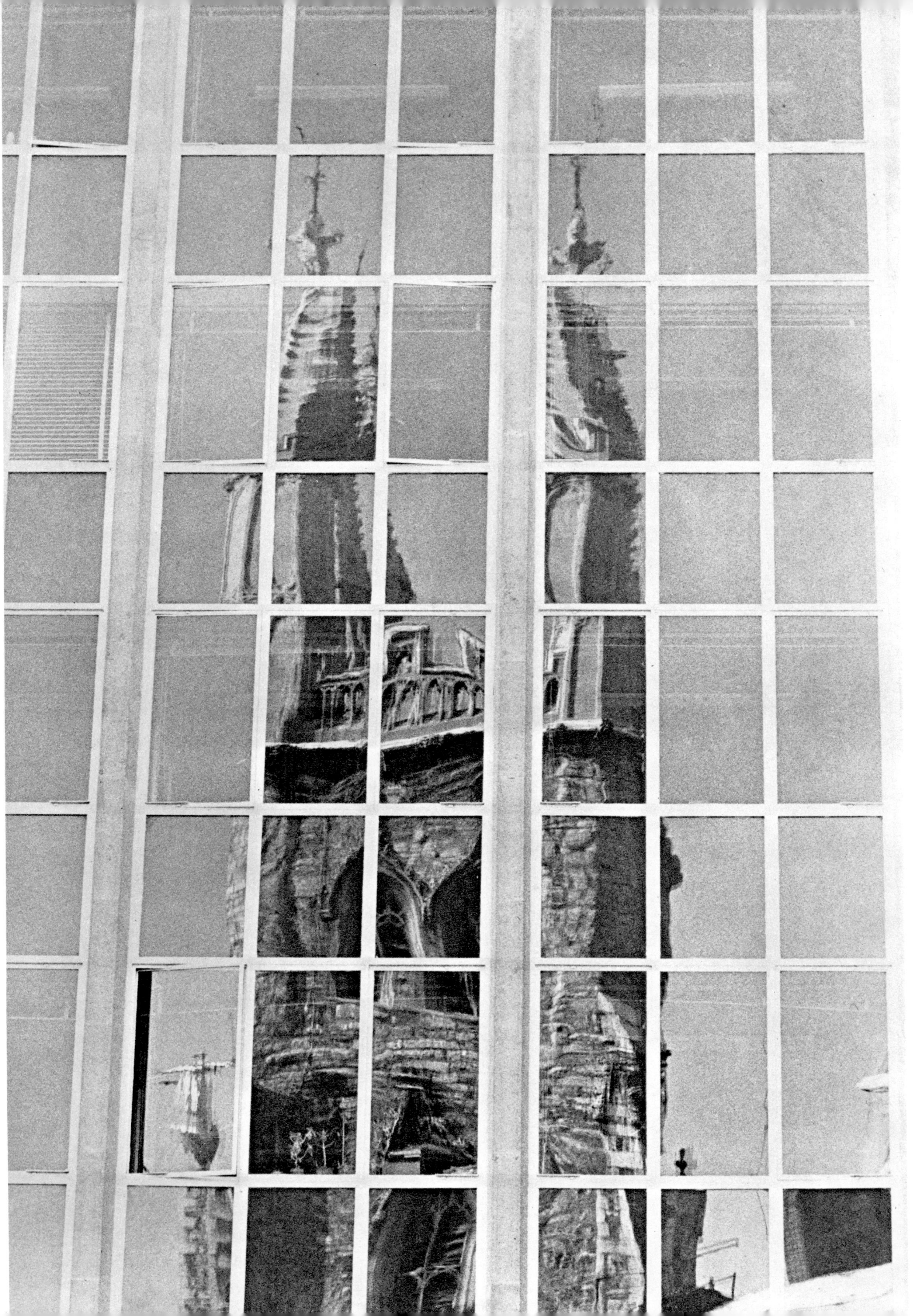

The Vickers Building on the north bank of the Thames. Its proper title is the Millbank Tower and it is considered London's most elegant tall building

Buses: London's characteristic red buses cross London Bridge

51

Buildings: the embankment from Waterloo Bridge. Scaffolding indicates long-term repairs to the dome of St. Paul's

Barges: the Thames is still a commercial waterway

Hotel doormen, at Grosvenor House (*above*) and at the Park Lane Hotel

London's policemen. *Above:* on traffic duty at Tower Bridge, and (*opposite*) in the Mall

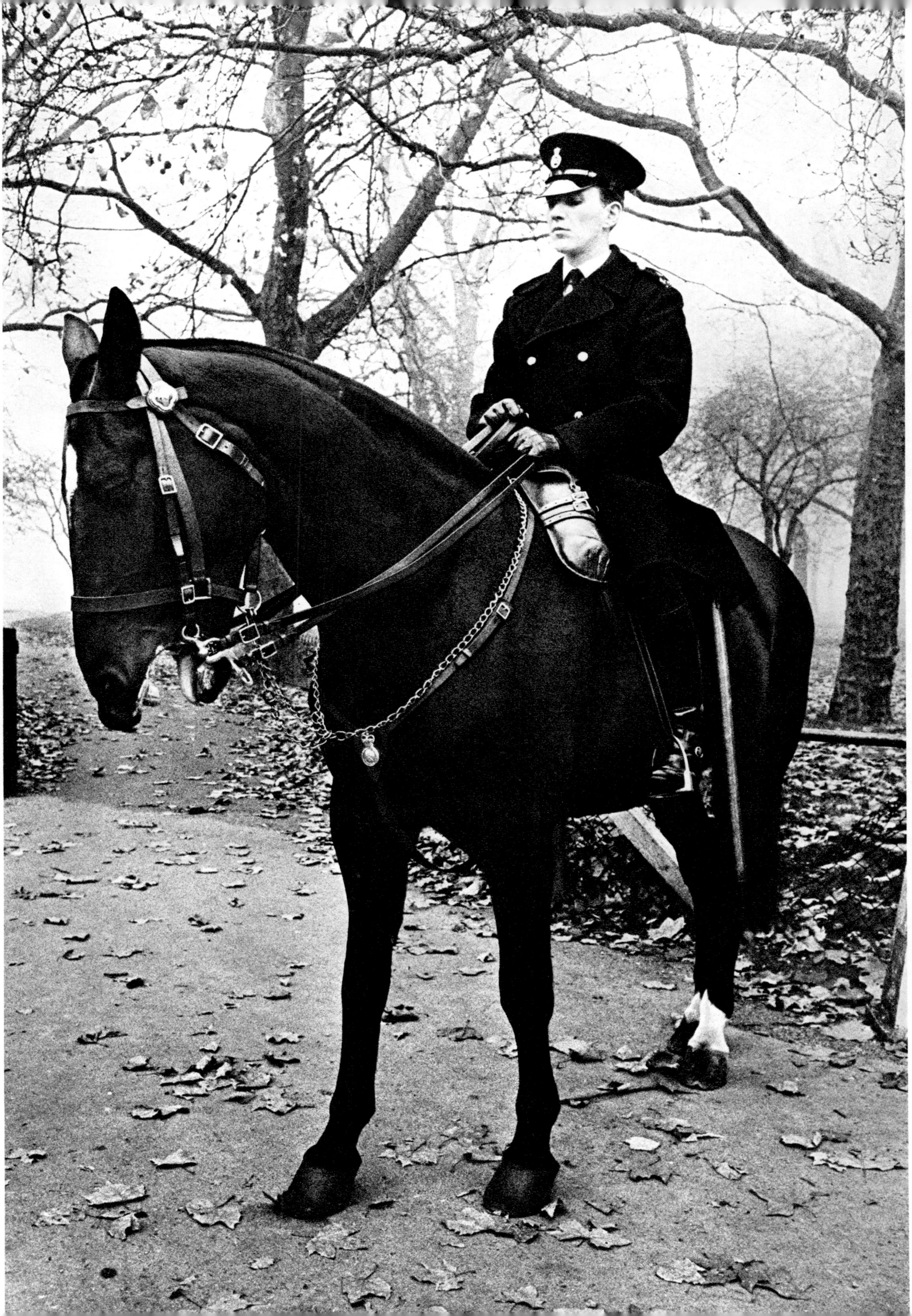

Fleet Street: a third of a mile of newspaper offices

Typically modern newspaper building, the Daily Mirror's headquarters at Holborn Circus

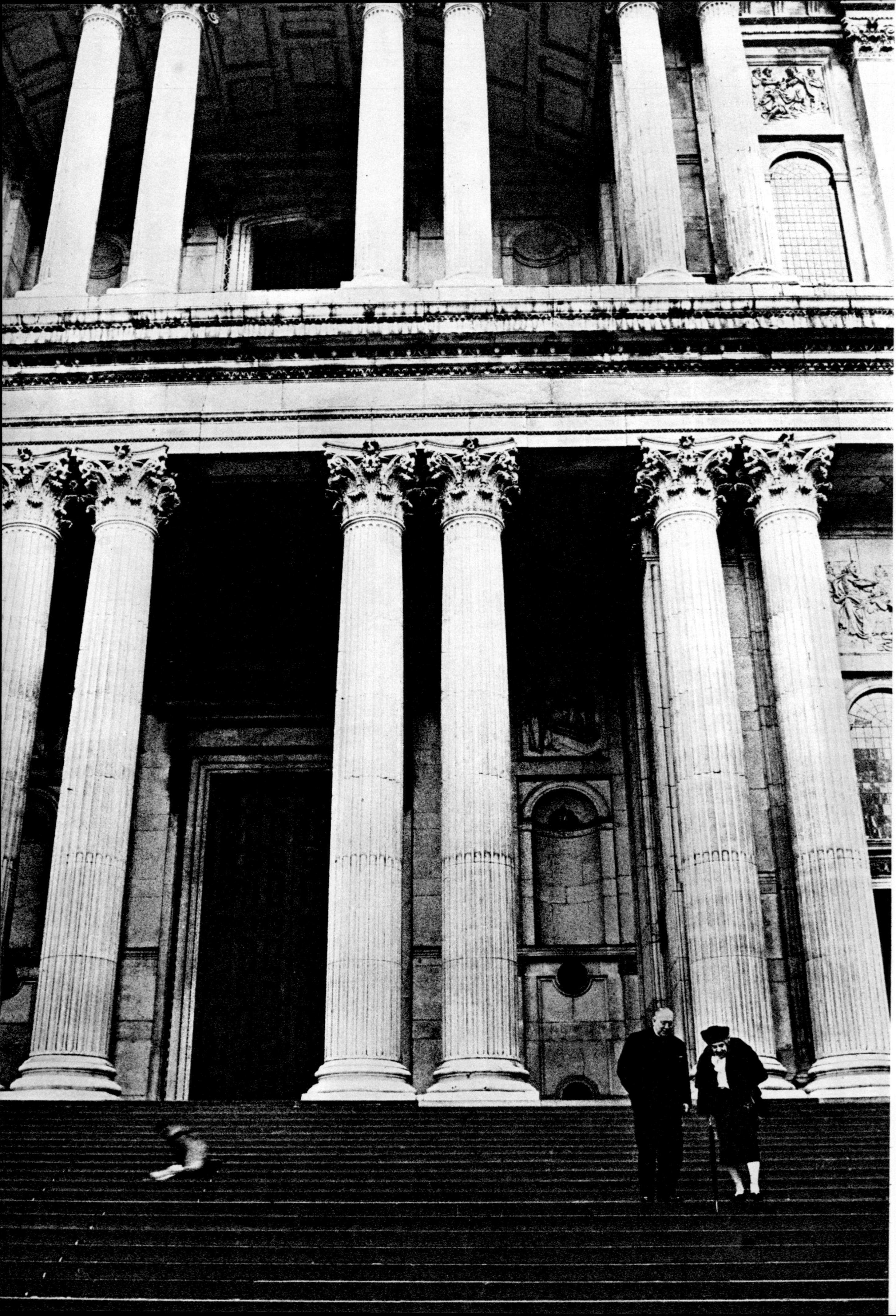

The Strand: one of the busiest streets in London, its name derived from the fact that it once ran beside the river as the main thoroughfare between Westminster and London. The church is St. Mary-le-Strand, now islanded by traffic. *Left*: main steps and west facade of St. Paul's Cathedral

Oxford Street: a straight line from Marble Arch to Tottenham Court Road, the main popular shopping area with a major concentration of clothing and department stores

HMV
BERLITZ
ACME FUR
CATCH A BUS
GO TO A CINEMA
CUV 107C
Darling
23

A central artery of Soho, the area associated with continental shops, a variety of clubs, restaurants, street markets, and where much of the popular music industry is located. Junction of Frith Street and Old Compton Street

A barber's shop in Highgate; the photographs in the window indicate the average Englishman's increased awareness of personal appearance

The Guildhall, or Hall of the Corporation of the City of London, heavily damaged by the great fire of 1666 and the blitz of 1940. To the left stands the church of St. Lawrence Jewry by Wren, official church of the City Corporation

Modern architecture in 18th century St. James's, the Economist Building a much praised concept of three towers built in 1964

The Shell Building on the south bank of the Thames is claimed to be the largest office block in Europe. It dominates most London views and can be seen from as far away as Hampton Court

Carlton House Terrace, with the Duke of York's column. On the Mall, once perhaps the most aristocratic place of residence in London – now almost entirely used as government offices

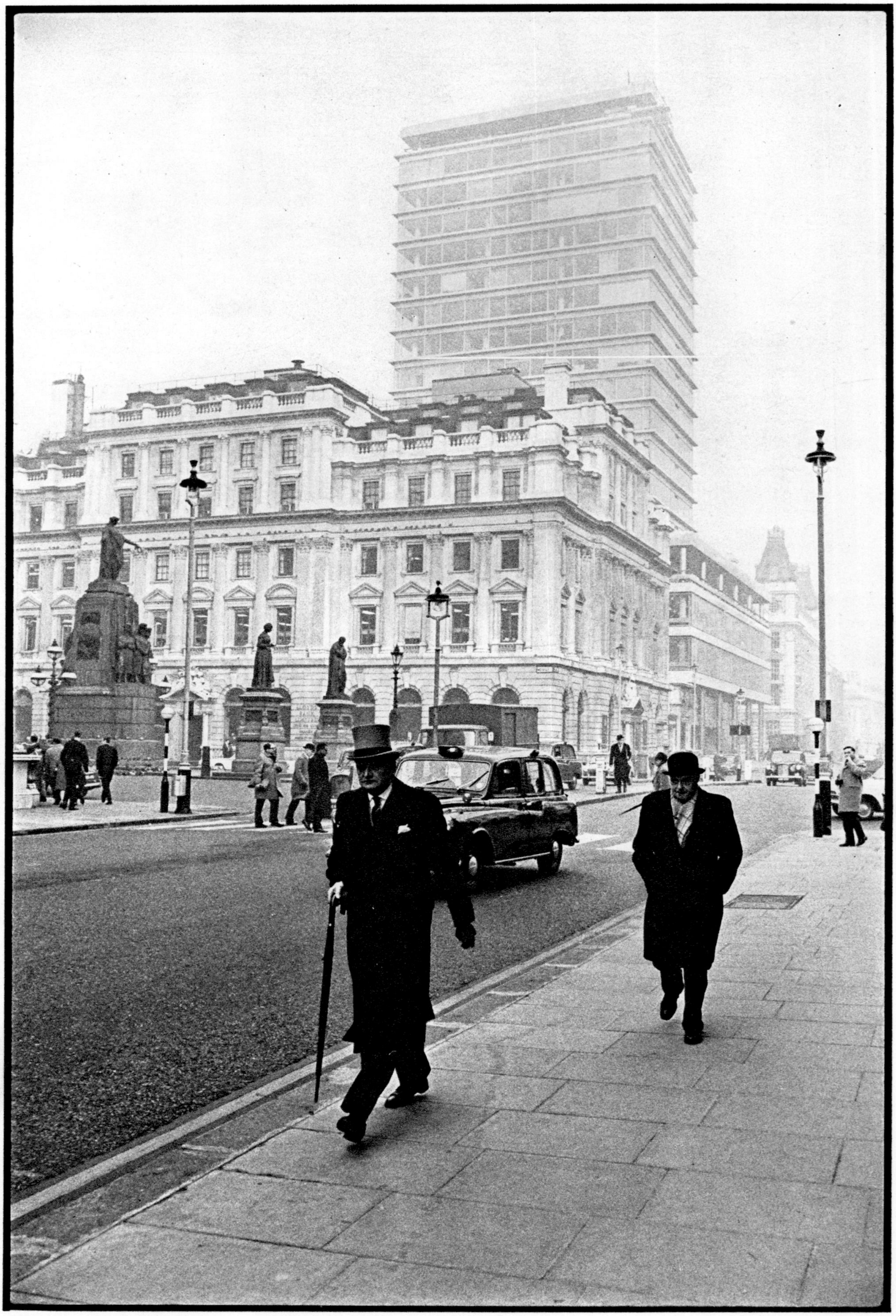

The American Embassy in Grosvenor Square, built in 1957-8 by Eero Saarinen. The 1695 square now is largely occupied by offices of the American government

Left: Pall Mall in St. James's, where many of London's exclusive clubs are found. Dominating is New Zealand House, an 18 storey tower with a celebrated view from its roof terrace

The Port of London. For sea-going ships the port ends at London Bridge and the Pool of London is just below Tower Bridge (*above right*). The docks stretch down to the Isle of Dogs where the river loops and contains the West India Dock and Millwall Outer Dock. Tilbury Docks are much further down river, some 26 miles below London Bridge. Warehouses and forests of cranes give the area its distinctive, romantic flavour

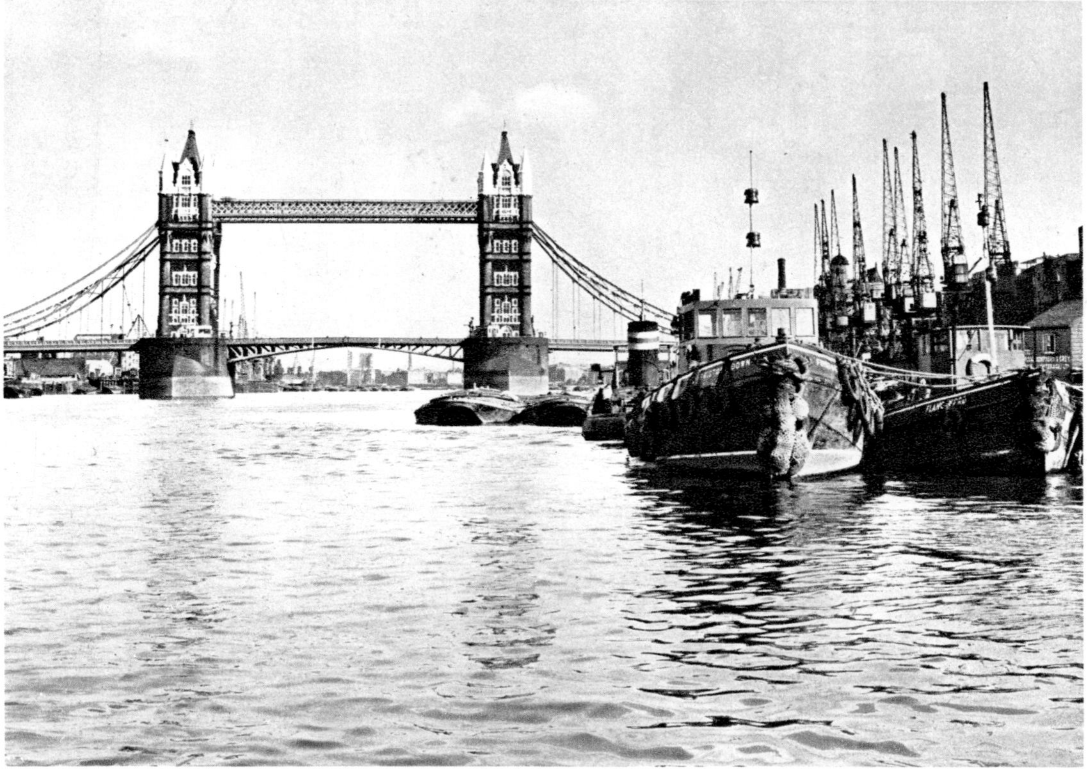

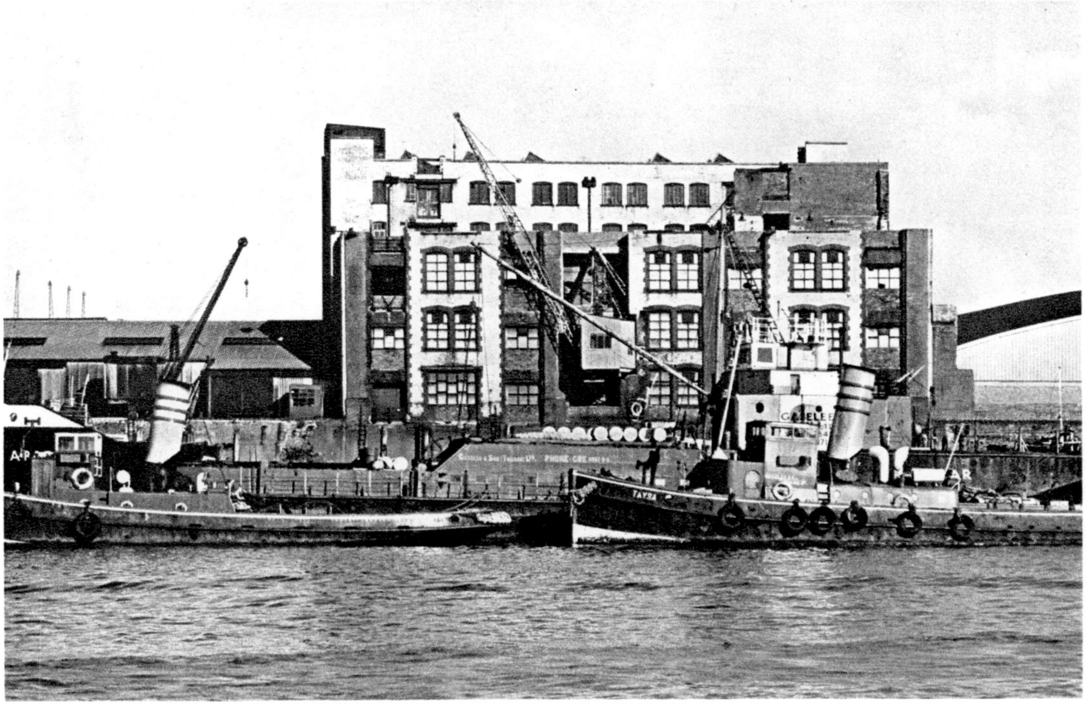

The Thames as it flows through the Chelsea area. *Right:* another waterway, the Regent's Canal, passes London Zoo

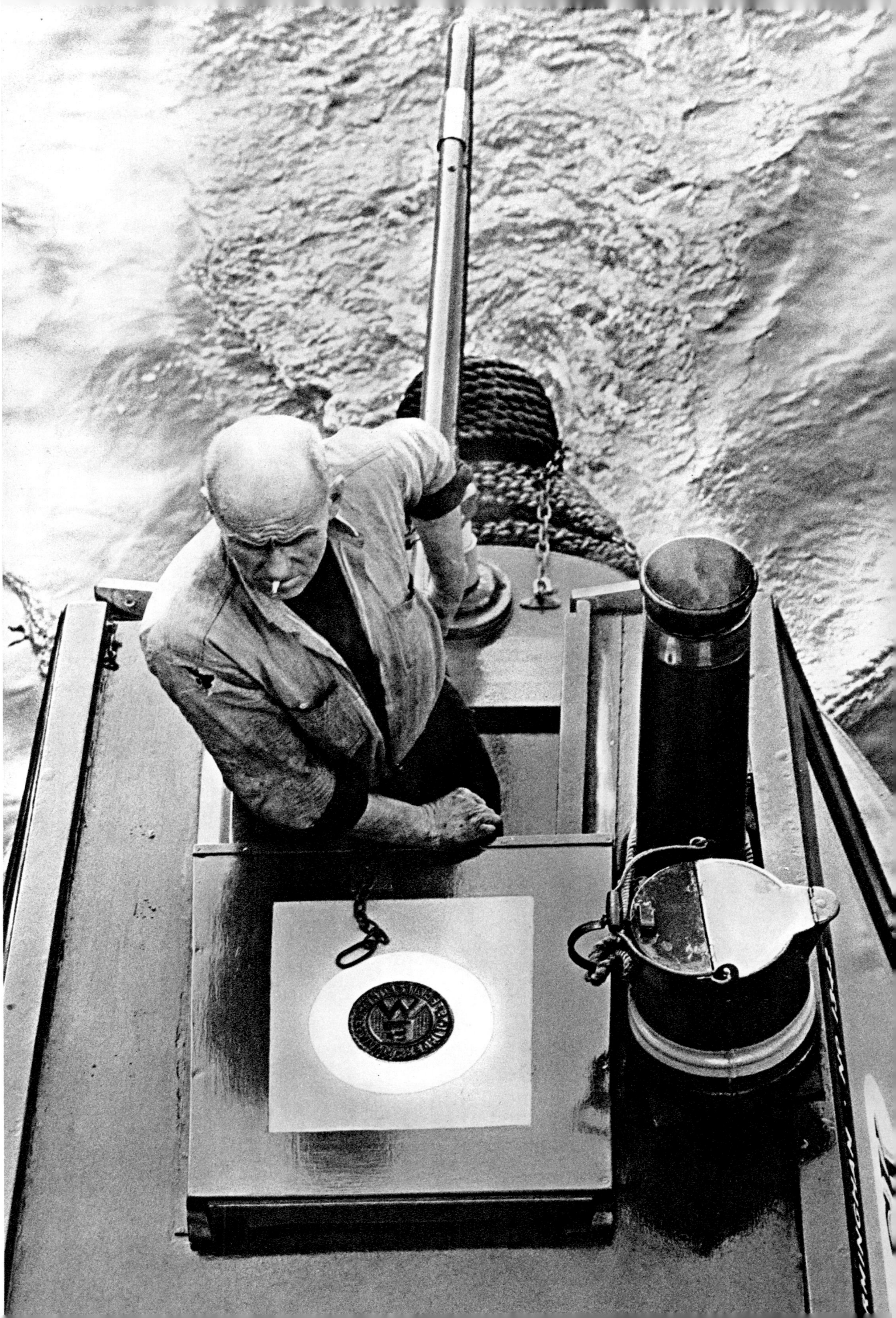

Bagpipers in the courtyard of Buckingham Palace

Outside the Guard Room at St. James's Palace

One of the attractive alleys in the Middle Temple, one of four Inns of Court, a quiet, part residential area between Fleet Street and the river

Trafalgar Square, scene of many varied rallies and meetings, also of general gaiety on New Year's Eve and where a Christmas tree is annually sited

The Banqueting Hall in Whitehall, by Inigo Jones, survivor of the extensive Palace of Whitehall

Right: unfamiliar view (from Westminster Abbey) of Big Ben, the east clock tower of the Houses of Parliament and named after Sir Benjamin Hall, first commissioner of works when the 13 ton bell was hung

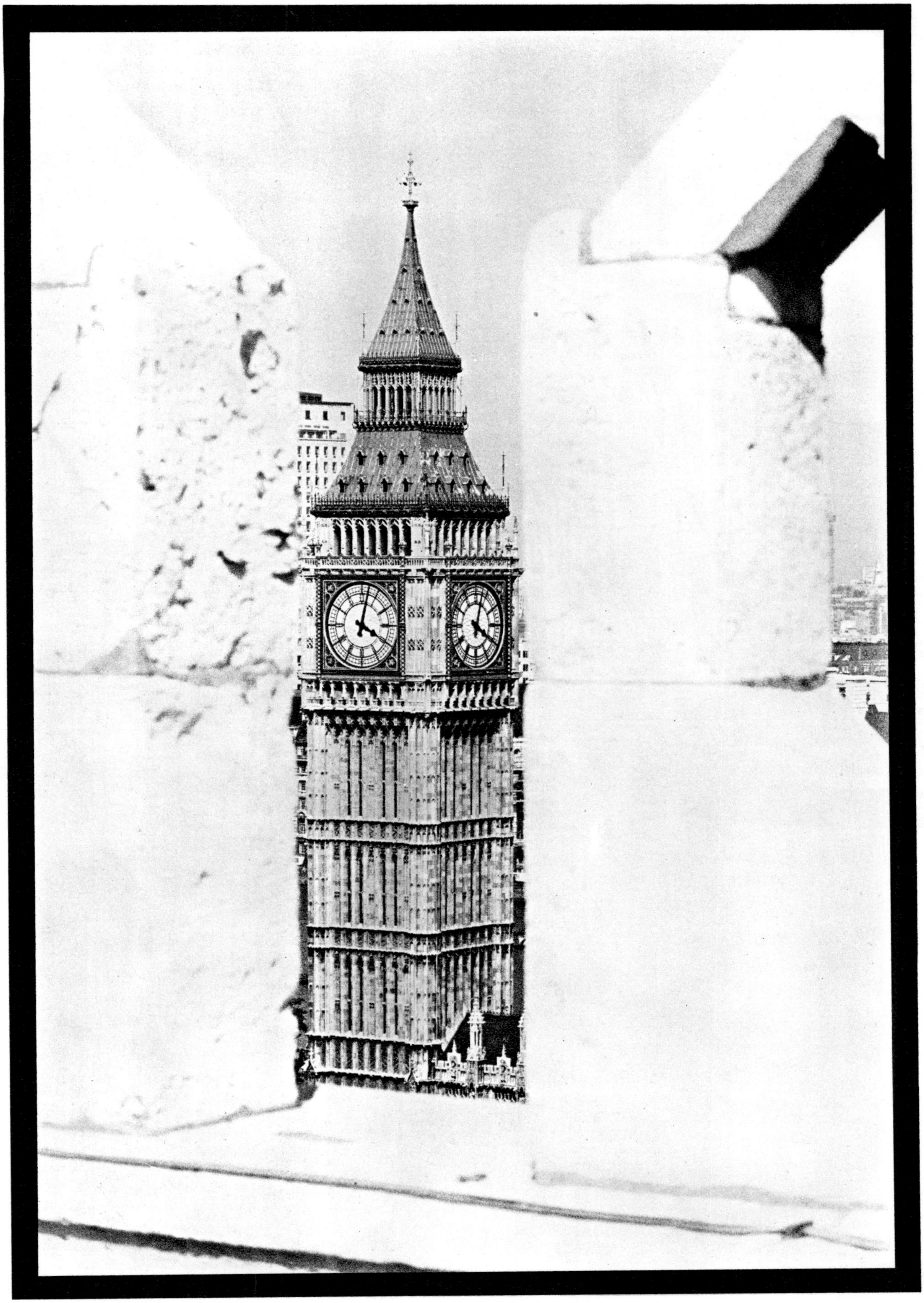

The House of Lords from Parliament Square. The spire stands over the central hall which separates the House of Lords from the House of Commons

Right: St. Martin's Lane with the Thorn Building as a contemporary backdrop for a busy street that contains theatres and colourful public houses and fringes Covent Garden

NEW
Oliver!
OLIVER!
APPLEFORD'S
CIDER VINEGAR
TO LET
INTERIOR &
STRUCTURAL
CLEANERS LTD
NELSON
CRANBOURNE

County Hall, headquarters of the Greater London Council with a river front of 750 feet

The Post Office tower and Tottenham Court Road. London's tallest building which apart from its functional use, has a revolving restaurant

Two celebrated views caught in the wide embraces of the fish-eye lens. *Above:* Tower Bridge and *right:* from the roof of the Savoy Hotel, the Shell Building dominates centrally. To the left is the City of London, to the right the towers of Westminster, both linked by the artery of the Thames

85

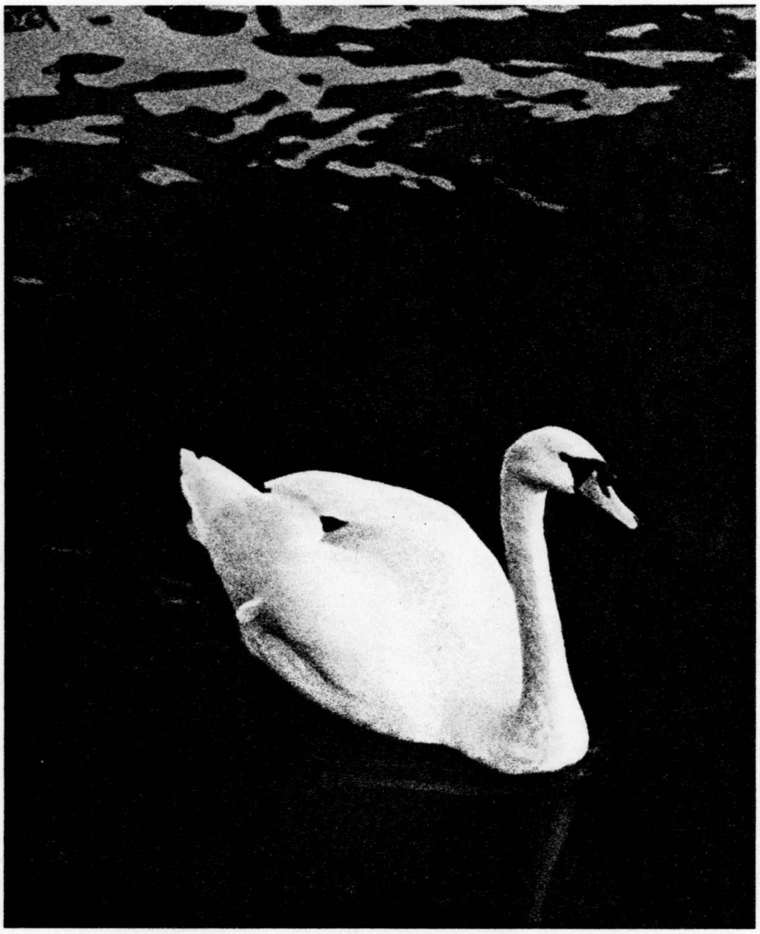

London Morning

When the rush hour is over, workers at their desks, trains and buses quiet, London changes character again. Morning is the time for shopping, in the elegant stores of the West End or in one of the bustling street markets. It is a time to watch patches of ceremony, the changing of the guard at Buckingham Palace and perhaps the bonus of a bigger occasion when the gates of the Palace are flung open and the state coach, attended by the splendour of the Household Cavalry, makes an appearance

Staple Inn, High Holborn. The timbered facade of the stretch of shops dates back to 1586 and is, though restored, the only survival of medieval London's street architecture

Petticoat Lane in London's East End. A street market which has the unusual distinction of being open on Sunday mornings

Major shopping streets impose their own atmosphere. A store window mirrors the crowds in Oxford Street

The curving quadrant of Regent Street, noted for its big stores, with annual Christmas decorations

Bond Street; its shops are synonymous with elegance, wealth, culture

Pipers pass the Victoria Memorial outside Buckingham Palace

Pageantry: Trooping the Colour, annual ceremony that takes place on the sovereign's official birthday, when one regiment of the guards presents its colour (that is, standard) to the Queen

93

Dressing in Jermyn Street: the colourful window of Turnbull & Asser

Eating in Jermyn Street: hams and cheeses at Paxton & Whitfield, provision merchants

Letter post: royal monogram on the pillar box dates back to the reign of Queen Victoria

Piccolo player of the band of the Welsh Guards at Buckingham Palace

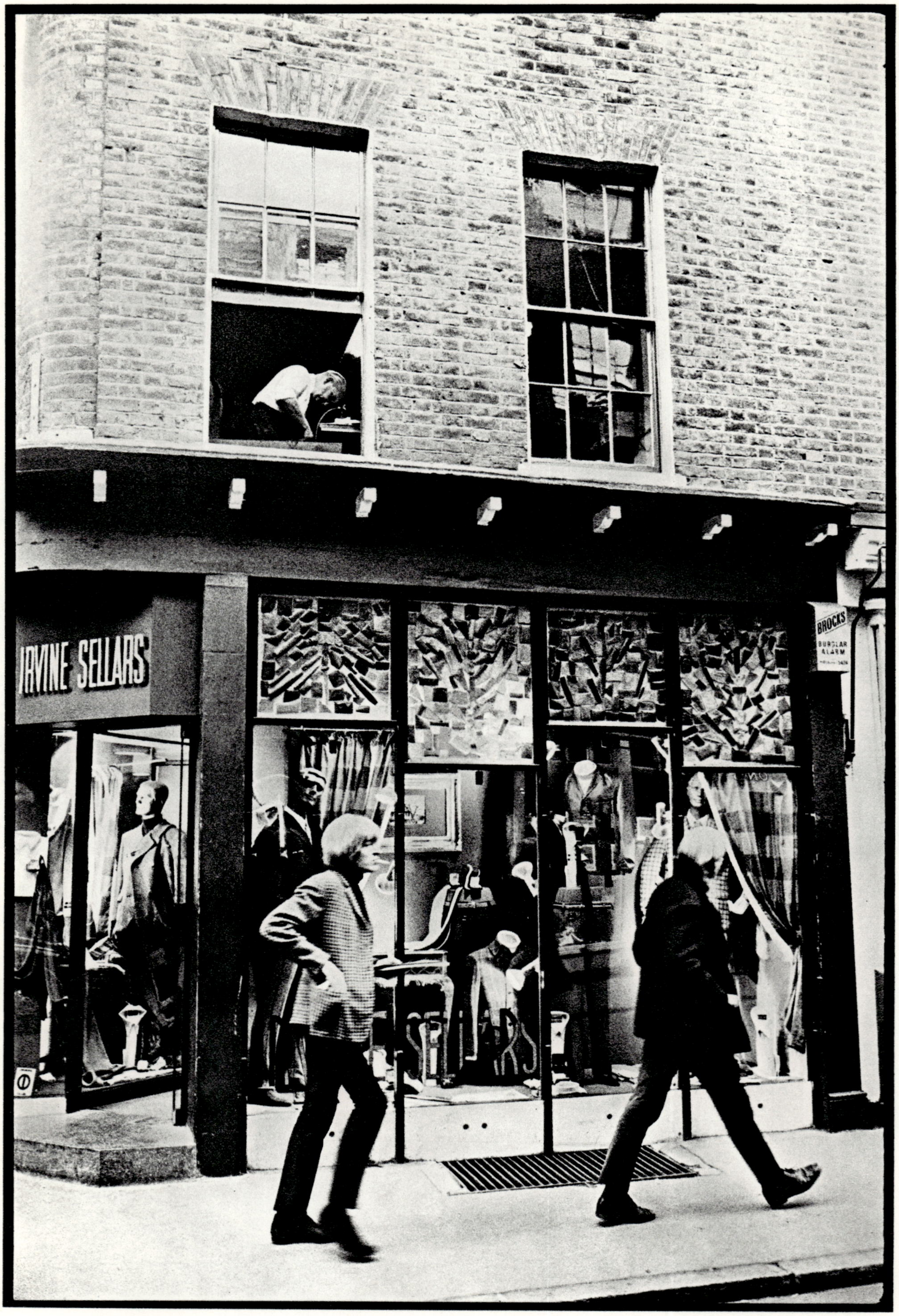
IRVINE SELLARS
BROCKS
BURGLAR ALARM
SELLARS

Carnaby Street. A narrow, and until 1957, ordinary street in Soho. Then John Stephens opened his first shop selling stylish clothes for young men. Others followed and the street is now the hub of the boutique industry and meeting place for youngsters

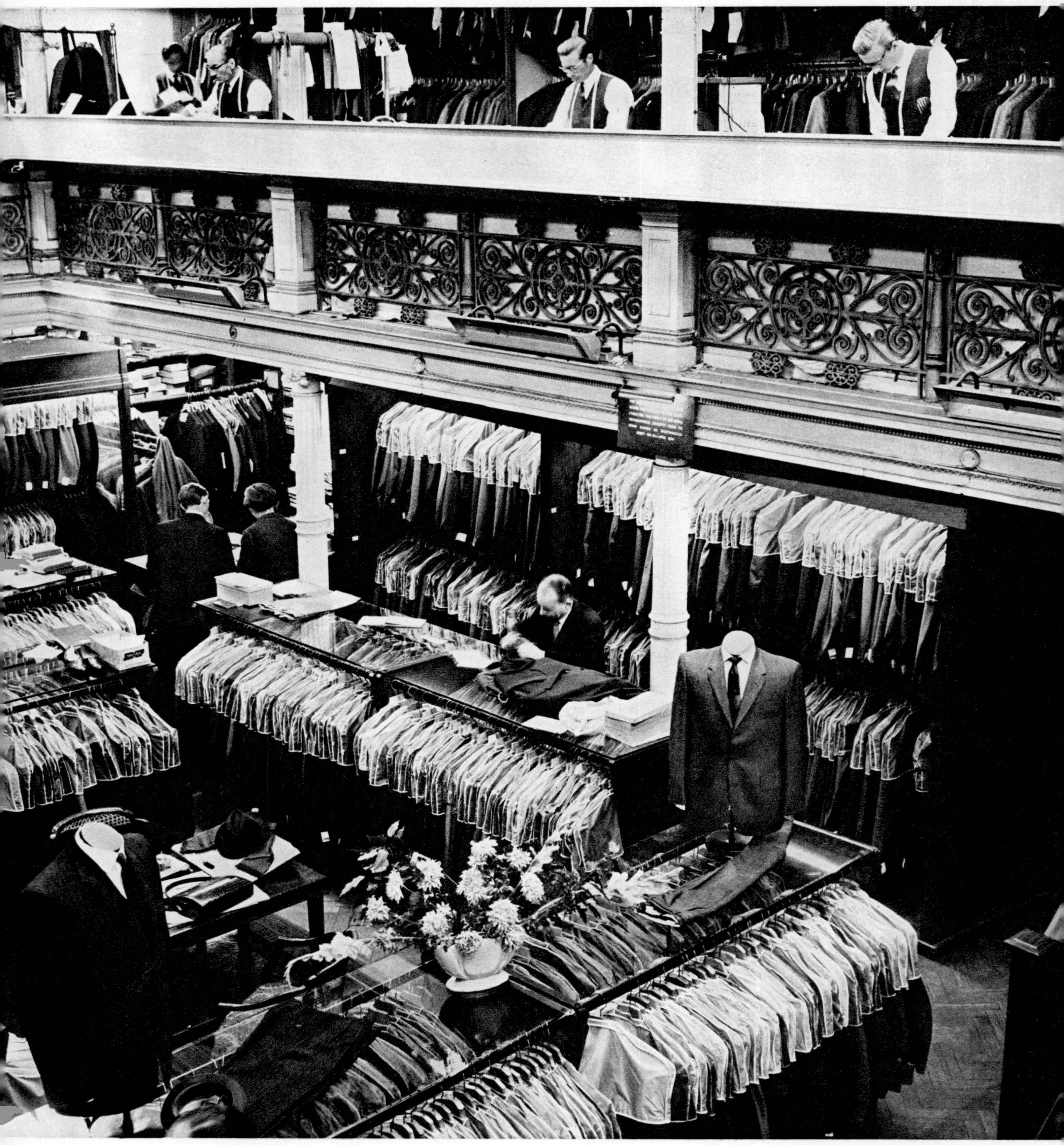

Two types of tailoring in Savile Row. *Above:* John Michael, typical of the new image London has acquired. *Left:* Hawkes the old-established bespoke tailor

For women: Biba's boutique in Kensington with its *art nouveau* decor. The clothes, at reasonable prices are indicative of the way in which young individuals (the proprietress is a model and fashion artist) have broken into the women's fashion industry

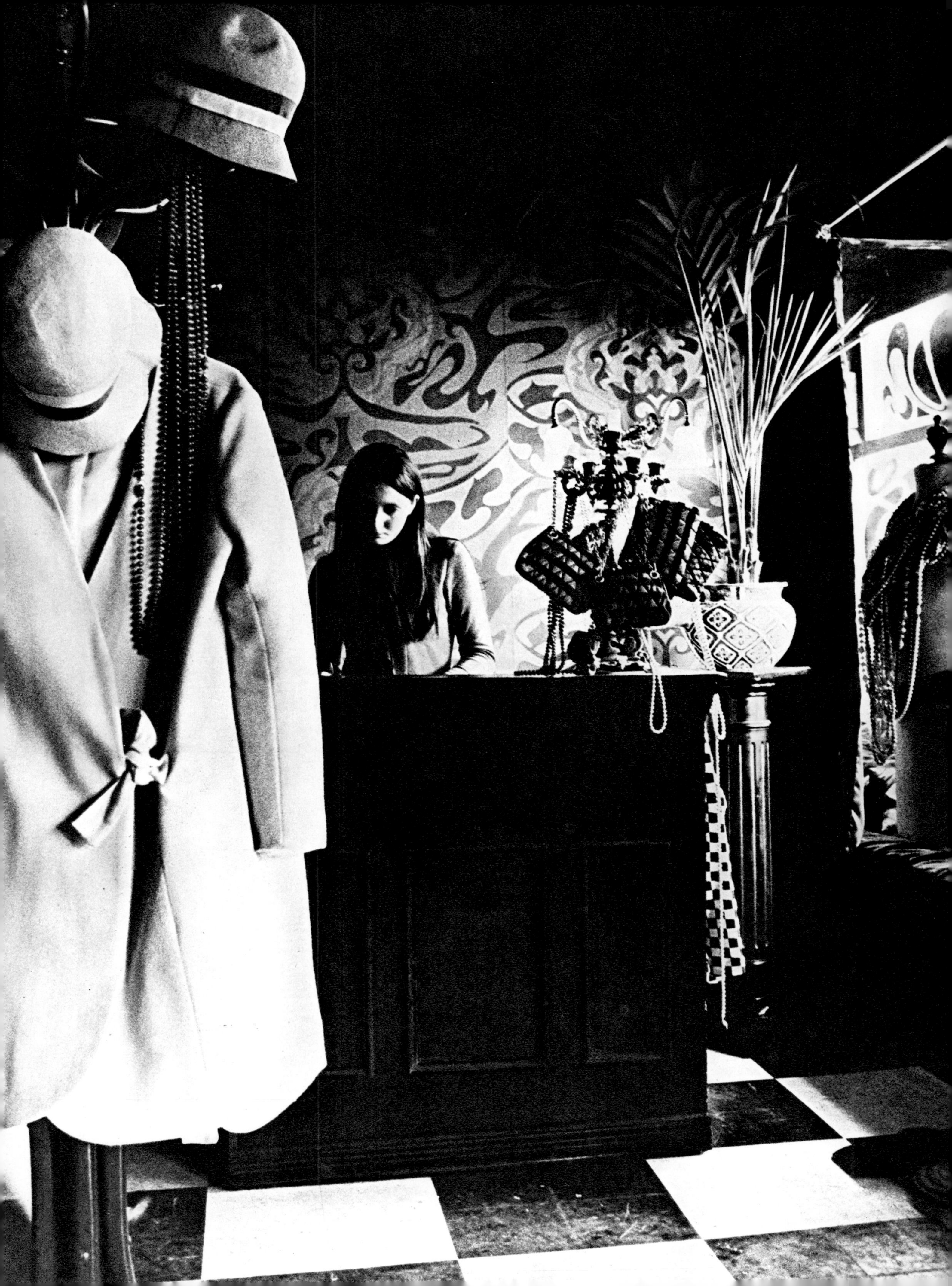

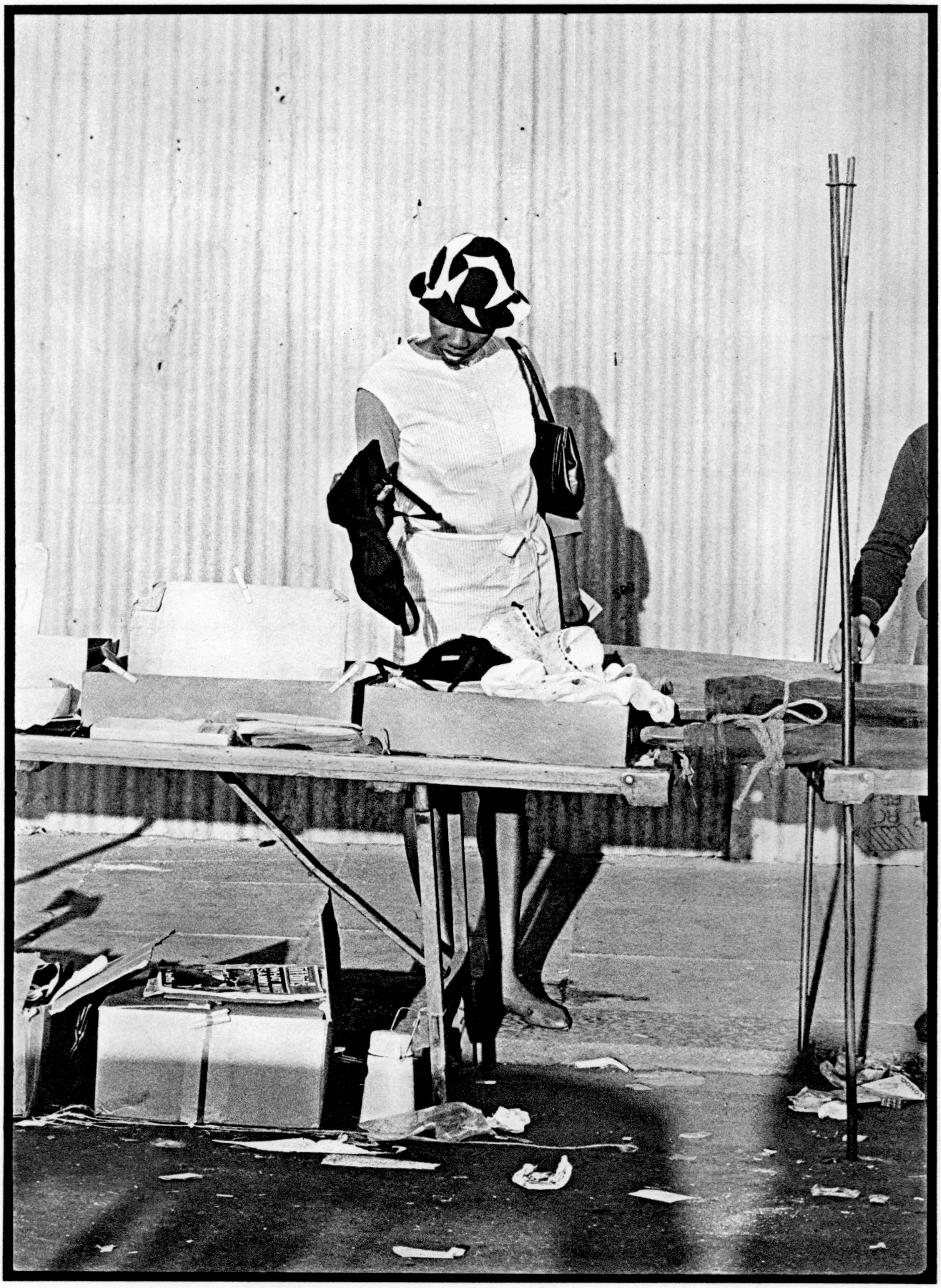

Portobello Road: one of London's most notable street markets, specialising in antiques, bric-a-brac and the flotsam of a century or more. Some stalls offer women's clothes, carts are used for bill posting, and while some of the area is being demolished some symbols remain, like the apothecary jar, sign of the chemist

105

Vanishing sight: the rag-and-bone man with horse and cart

Opposite: reclaiming vanishing sights, buying up remembrances of the past in Portobello Road street market

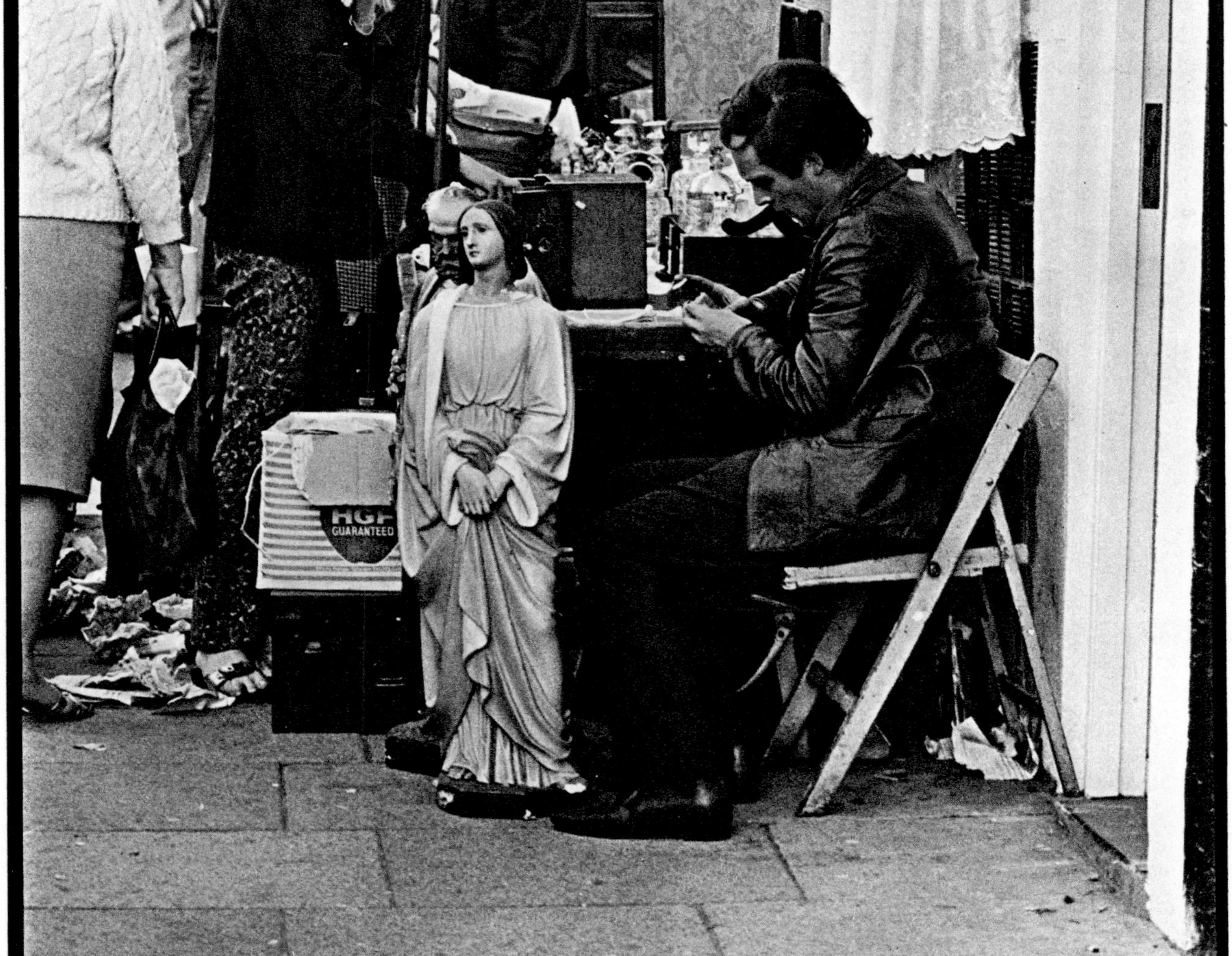
GUARANTEED

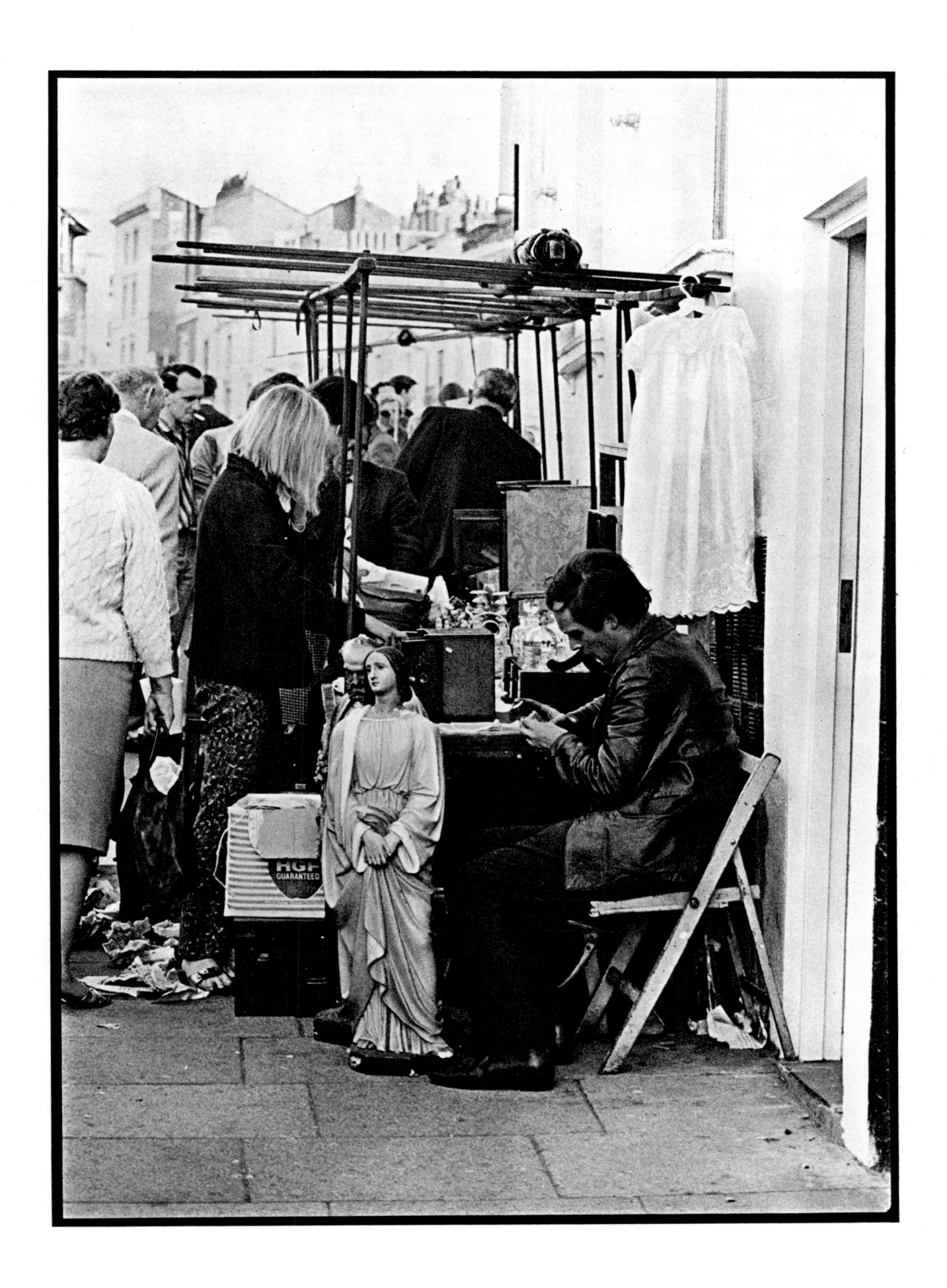

The shop of James Lock & Co., the hatters of St. James's which was established in the 18th century

London wedding. In St. James's Gardens, a quiet square in Holland Park

Street market in Soho; Berwick Street just off Shaftesbury Avenue, notable for fruit and vegetables

Street market in Islington; Camden Passage where bombed sites are used to accommodate antique stalls

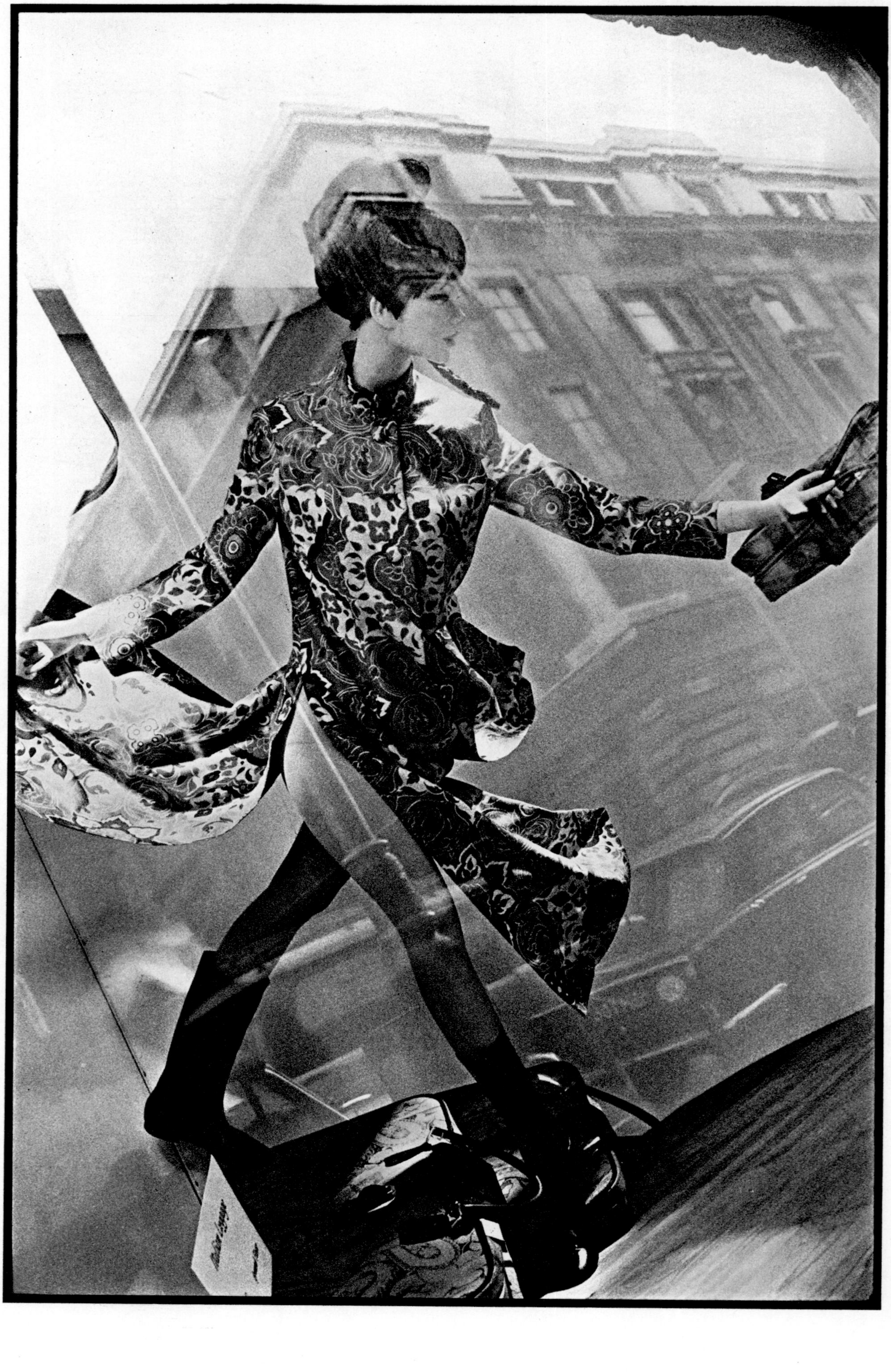

Fish counter in the food hall at Harrods in Knightsbridge, possibly the most famous department store in the world

Left: model girl in a window display at Liberty's in Regent Street, noted for prints such as the dummy is wearing

Hatchards' bookshop in Piccadilly

Bond Street: Asprey's the jewellers

An auction at Sotheby & Co. Here a sale of fine French glass paperweights. Even without money to buy, visitors can observe

The Queen drives from Buckingham Palace for the State Opening of Parliament attended by a troop of the Household Cavalry

By the Duke of York's column on the Mall, a man salutes the Household Cavalry as they pass on their way to the Changing of the Guard ceremony. There are two regiments of the Household Cavalry, the Life Guards and the Royal Horse Guards

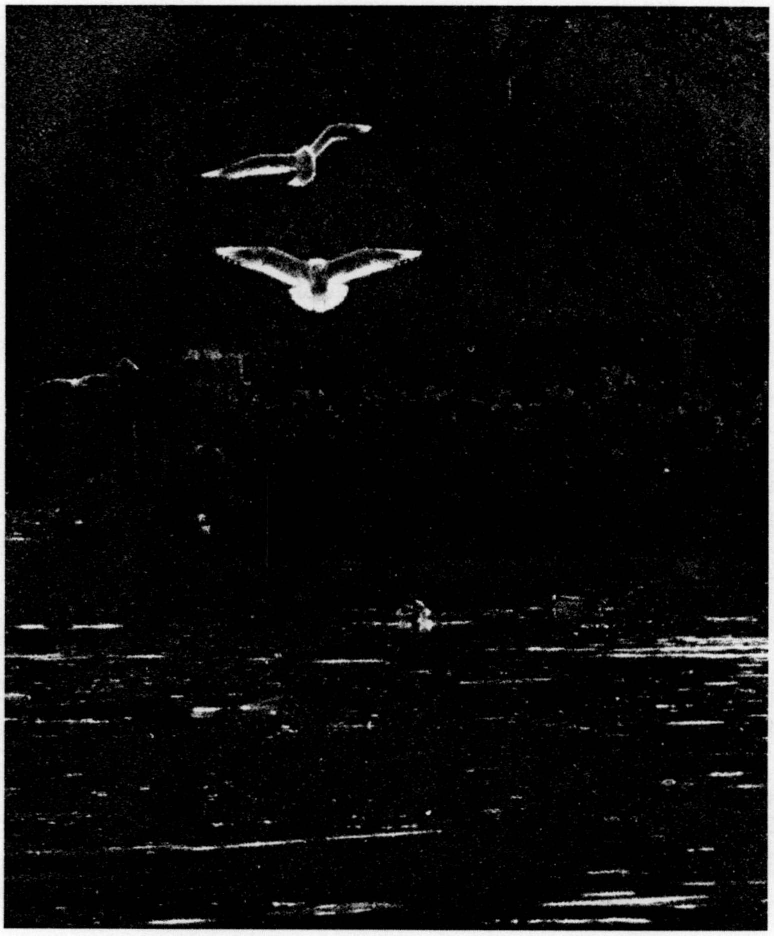

London Living

London is essentially a residential city. No matter what particular function any given area has, there remain private residences. Many of the large, aristocratic houses have now been demolished or turned into embassies and offices. But enough remain. And the streets of houses in various parts of London have their own characteristics of style and usage

Buckingham Palace, the residence of the Queen. Part of the palace – which reached its present form in 1825 – was damaged during the war, but the relevant wing was rebuilt to form the Queen's Gallery where the public can see regular exhibitions of items from the royal collection – the greatest private art collection in the world. *Right:* the Queen Mother's car arriving at her residence, Clarence House

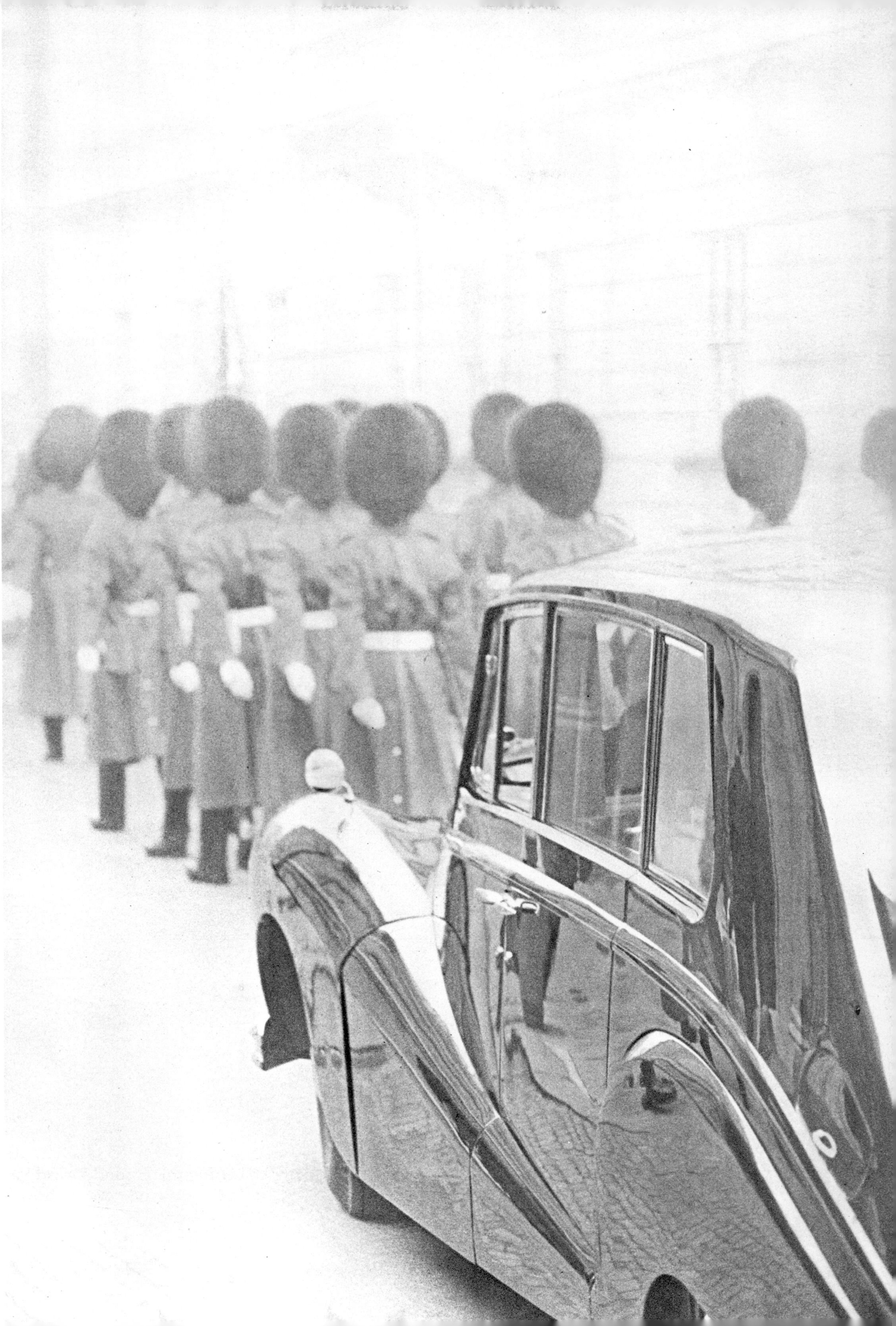

Street in Bethnal Green

Opposite: London Wall; an area that suffered heavy damage during the Second World War, now reaching the final stages of development with new office blocks and pedestrian bridges.
Below: Gracechurch Street in the City of London

123

London Wall: the street follows the line of London's Roman wall, part of which has been incorporated into the rebuilding. This fragment is in the once churchyard of St. Alphage
Opposite: what the modern architect is replacing – an East London street

Drink
TIZER
The Appetizer
Roll A1 LIGHT
Coca-Cola
R·WHITE'S
SOFT DRINKS
SOLD HERE
Kensitas
are here!
CHURCHMANS
NOW 4'6
FLING
FRESHENS and FORTIFIES!
SOFT
R.WHITE'S
DRINKS
Kensitas
are here!
BOAR'S HE
TOBA
FOR CIGAR
TARZAN
THE APE MAN
CLIFF R
SUM
HOL
PHILIP CAREY

The Moorish influence in lavish domestic architecture. House in Kensington Palace Gardens, known as Millionaire Row, now the Saudi-Arabian Embassy

Three of London's hotels; the Dorchester in Park Lane (*above left*), the Carlton Tower in Cadogan Place, Chelsea (*above right*) and the Europa, just off Grosvenor Square (*top*)

The Imperial Hotel, Russell Square an example of elaborate hotel architecture, now demolished in favour of a new building

The Hilton Hotel in Park Lane

Eaton Square, part of Belgravia a spaciously-planned aristocratic area built about 1830. Still largely residential and coveted

Typical 19th century development of South London seen from a train

Harley Street, part of the fashionable complex of streets to the north of Oxford Street. This one is associated with the medical profession, as many doctors have their practices there

Canonbury Square in Islington, an area of residential contrast

Park Crescent built in 1812 by John Nash and recently restored. Note the street furniture: a horse trough and parking meters

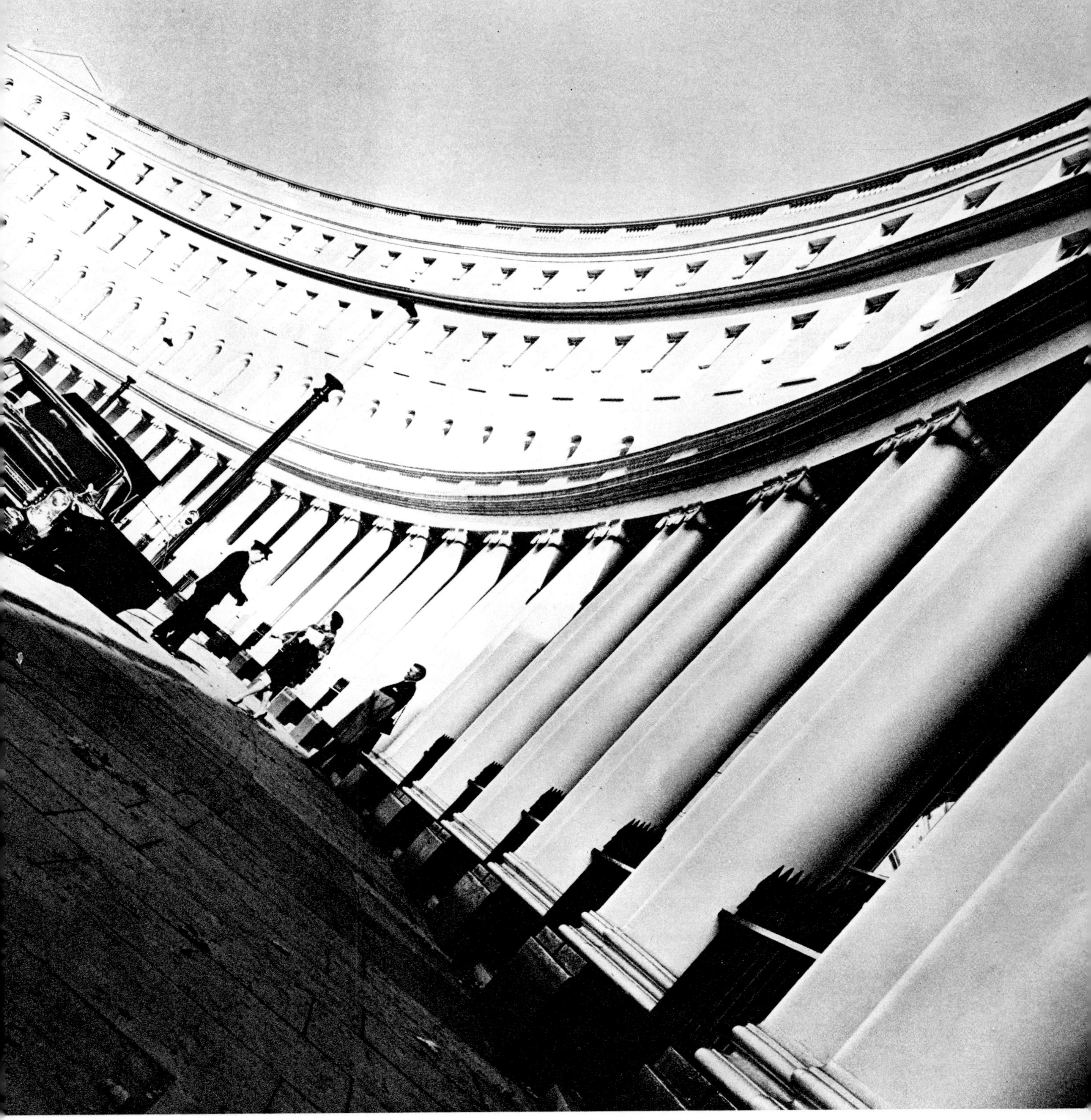

Dr. Samuel Johnson's house in Gough Square, a tiny court just off the north side of Fleet Street

Charles Dickens' house in Doughty Street, Bloomsbury. The basement contains a replica of the kitchen at Dingley Dell *The Pickwick Papers*

Kensington Palace where Queen Victoria was born and lived until she succeeded to the throne in 1837. Today part of the palace is the residence of Princess Margaret and Lord Snowdon

Noel Road, Islington. The gardens of the houses end at the canal bank and the stretch is locally known as the Hanging Gardens of Islington

Some Londoners live on the river; a group of houseboats off Cheyne Walk in Chelsea

Street in north Kensington

Right: Stockwell, south London; a tramp carries his possessions around on a flat-tyred bicycle

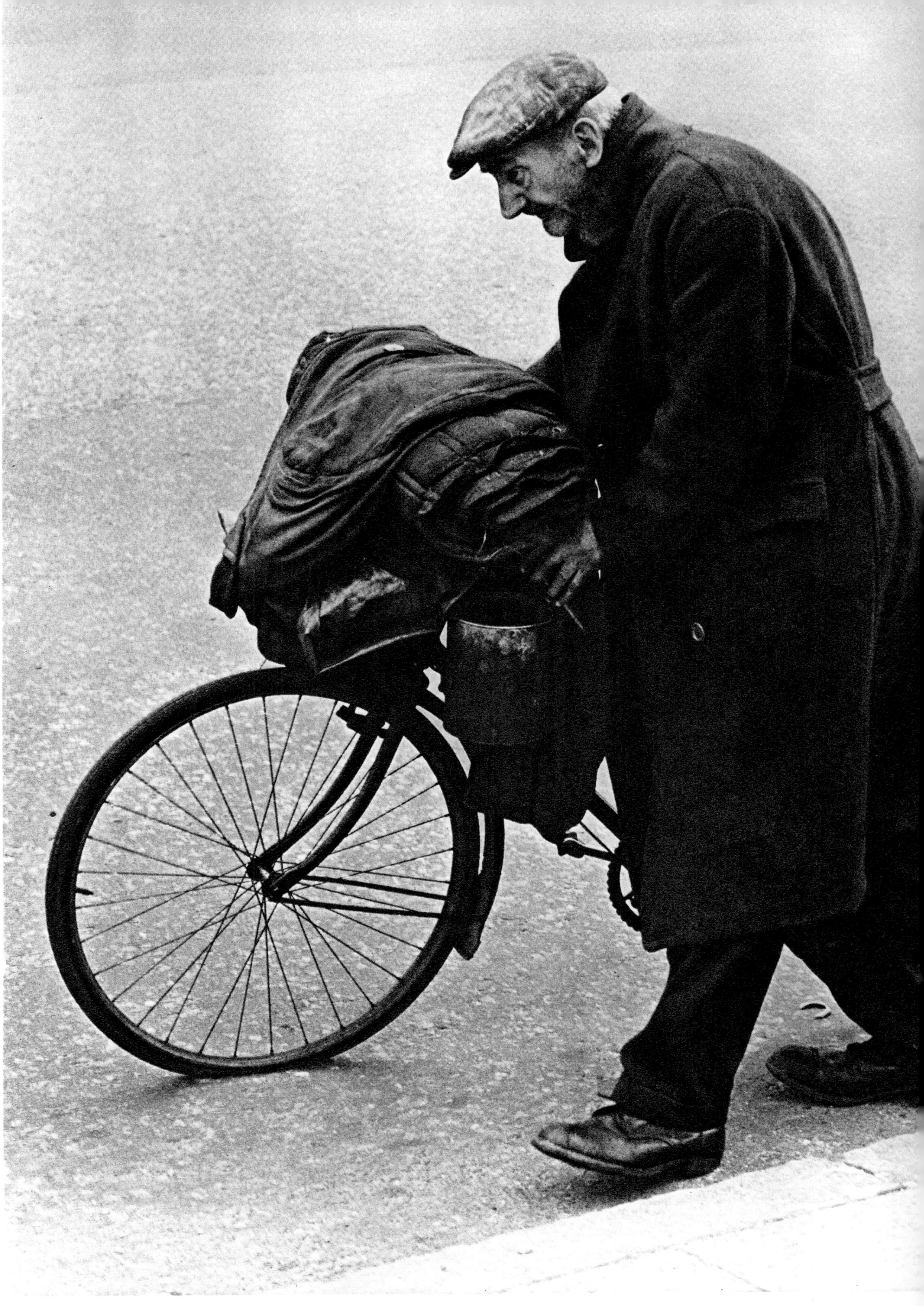

The Albany (or just Albany) a block of suites of rooms (or sets) just off Piccadilly. Byron and Macaulay are among those who have lived there; today's residents are also illustrious

No. 10 Downing Street, official residence of the Prime Minister. No. 11 is the official residence of the Chancellor of the Exchequer, no. 12 is the Government Whip's office

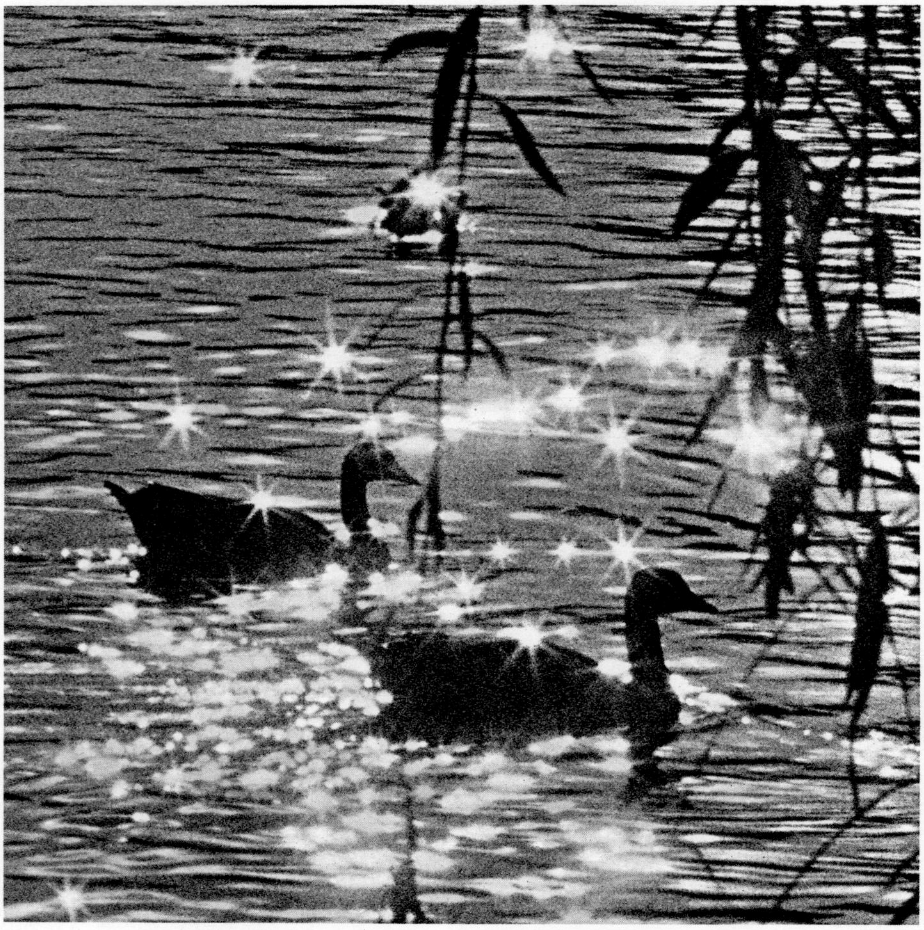

London Afternoon

The afternoon has a quality of its own. It is a time for leisure, but productive leisure. A time to look at the fine city churches, to visit art galleries, museums, the zoo, the Tower of London. There are other, less serious-minded attractions – like the many fairs, occasional sporting events, or just strolling about

The Elgin Marbles in the British Museum

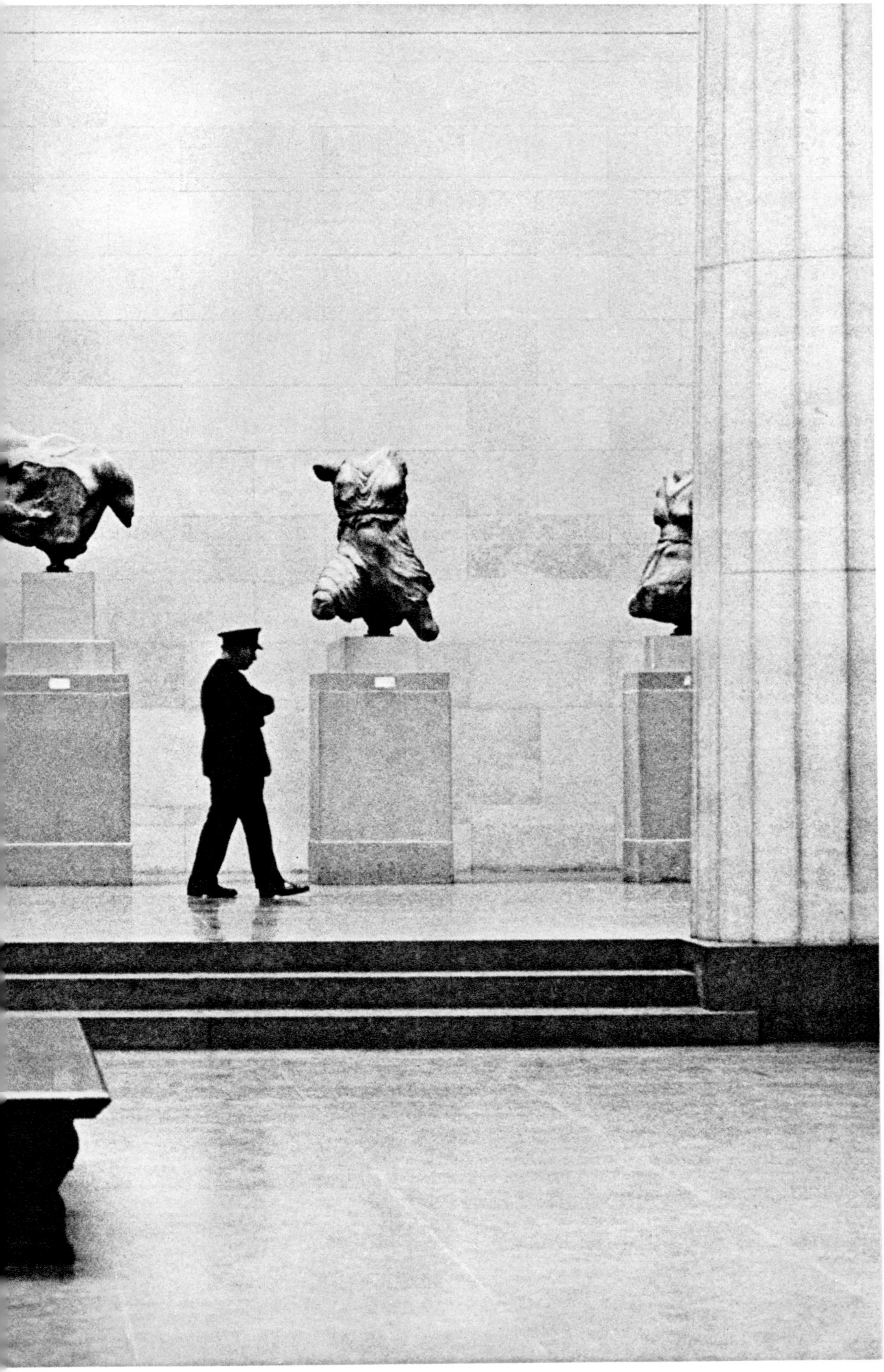

Children with fishing nets explore the edge of the Round Pond in Kensington Gardens

One of the most celebrated London views – the domes, spires and towers of Whitehall seen from the bridge in St. James's Park

Fun fair: at Battersea, a permanent amusement opened for the Festival of Britain

Fun fair: at Hampstead. On the dodgem cars at an itinerant fair that settles on the heath during holiday weekends

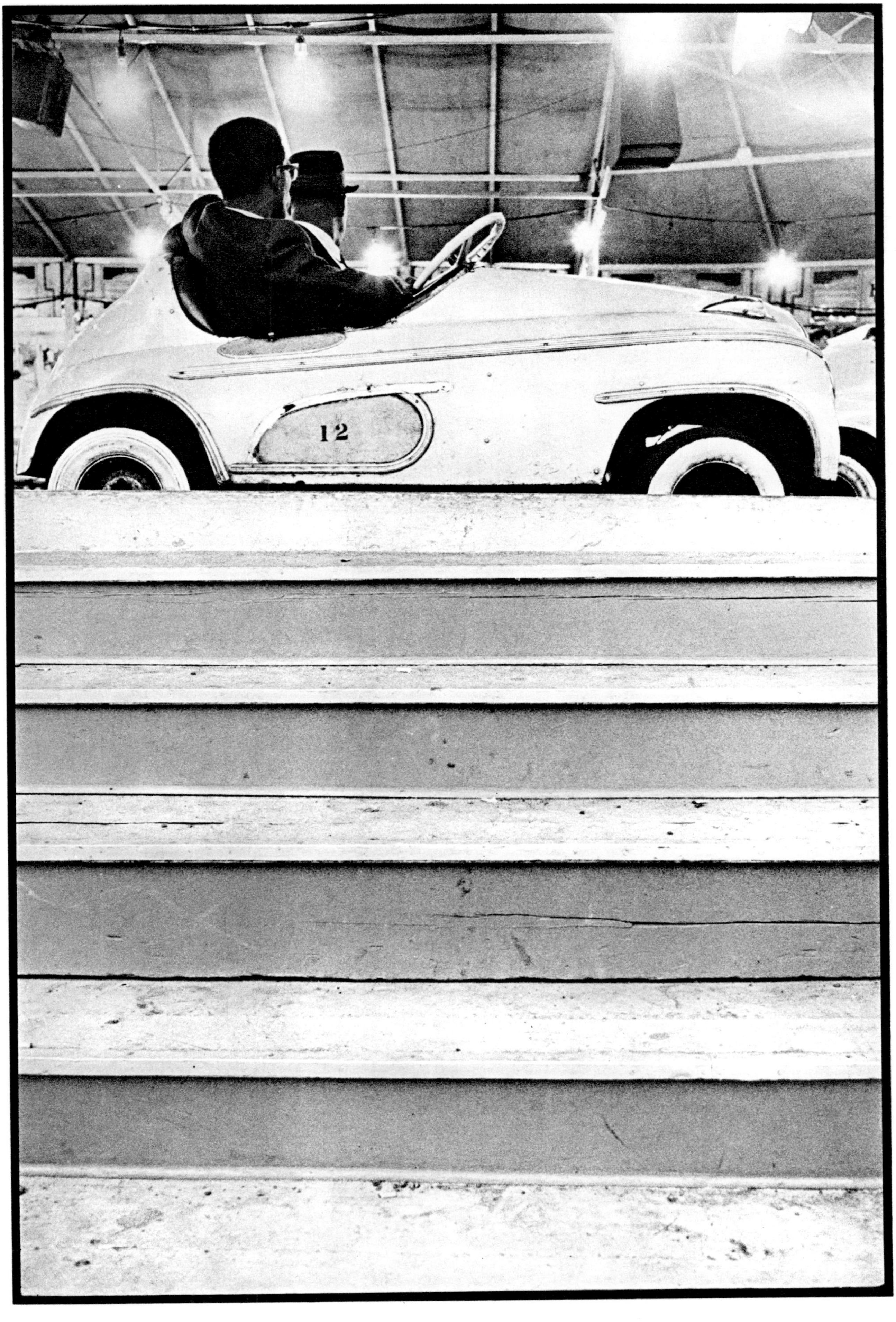
12

Hammersmith Bridge; afternoon sun points its distinctive shape

Blackfriars railway bridge; on the river, the training ships Discovery, Chrysanthemum and President

Dodgem cars on Hampstead Heath

Saturday afternoon is, for many, dedicated to football. South Londoners cross Battersea Bridge to Stamford Bridge, Chelsea's ground

St. Andrew's church Holborn, built by Wren in 1684, destroyed in 1940, rebuilt 1960

Opposite top: St. Pancras church was built in a variety of styles inspired by Greece and included this copy of the Erectheum in Athens. *Right:* Hampton Court Palace: bridge and gatehouse

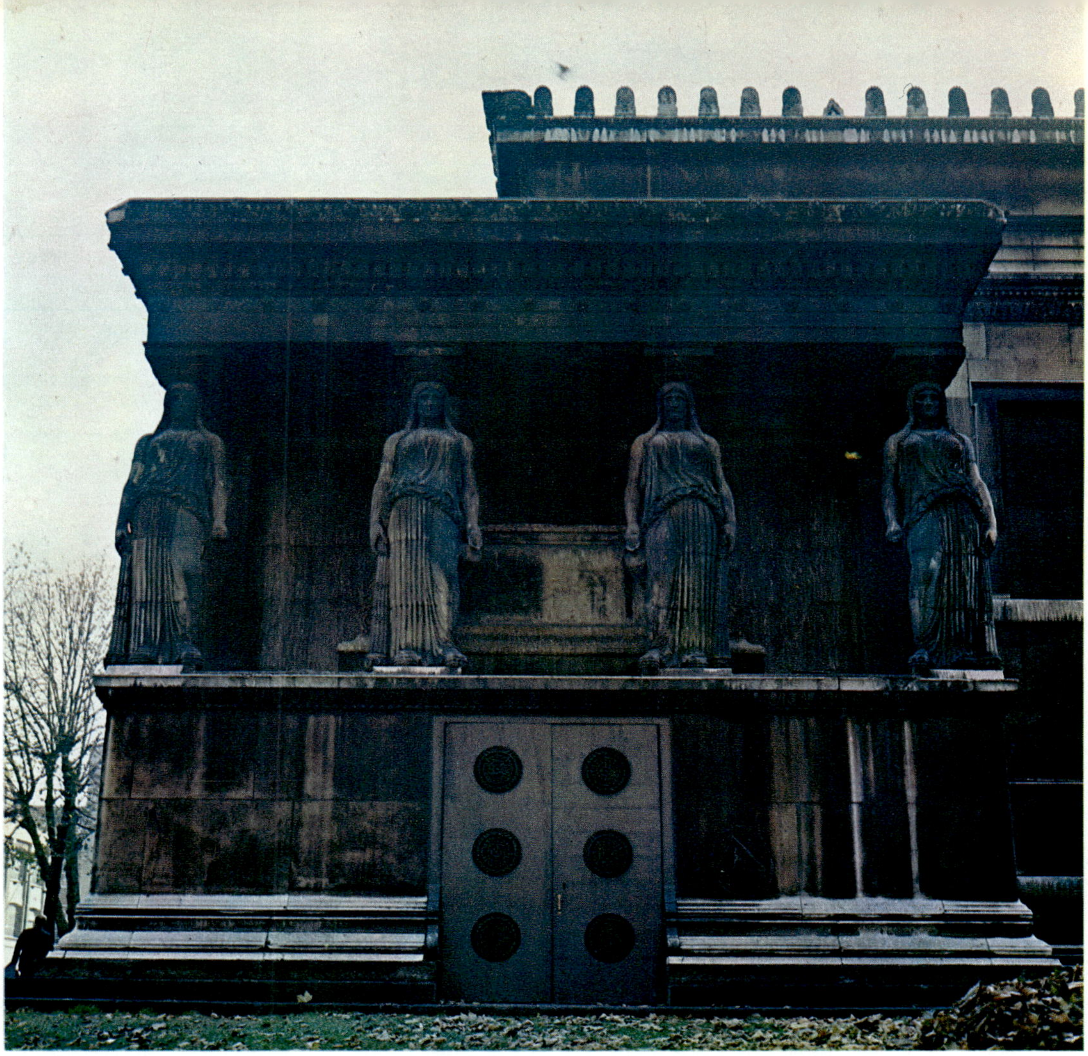

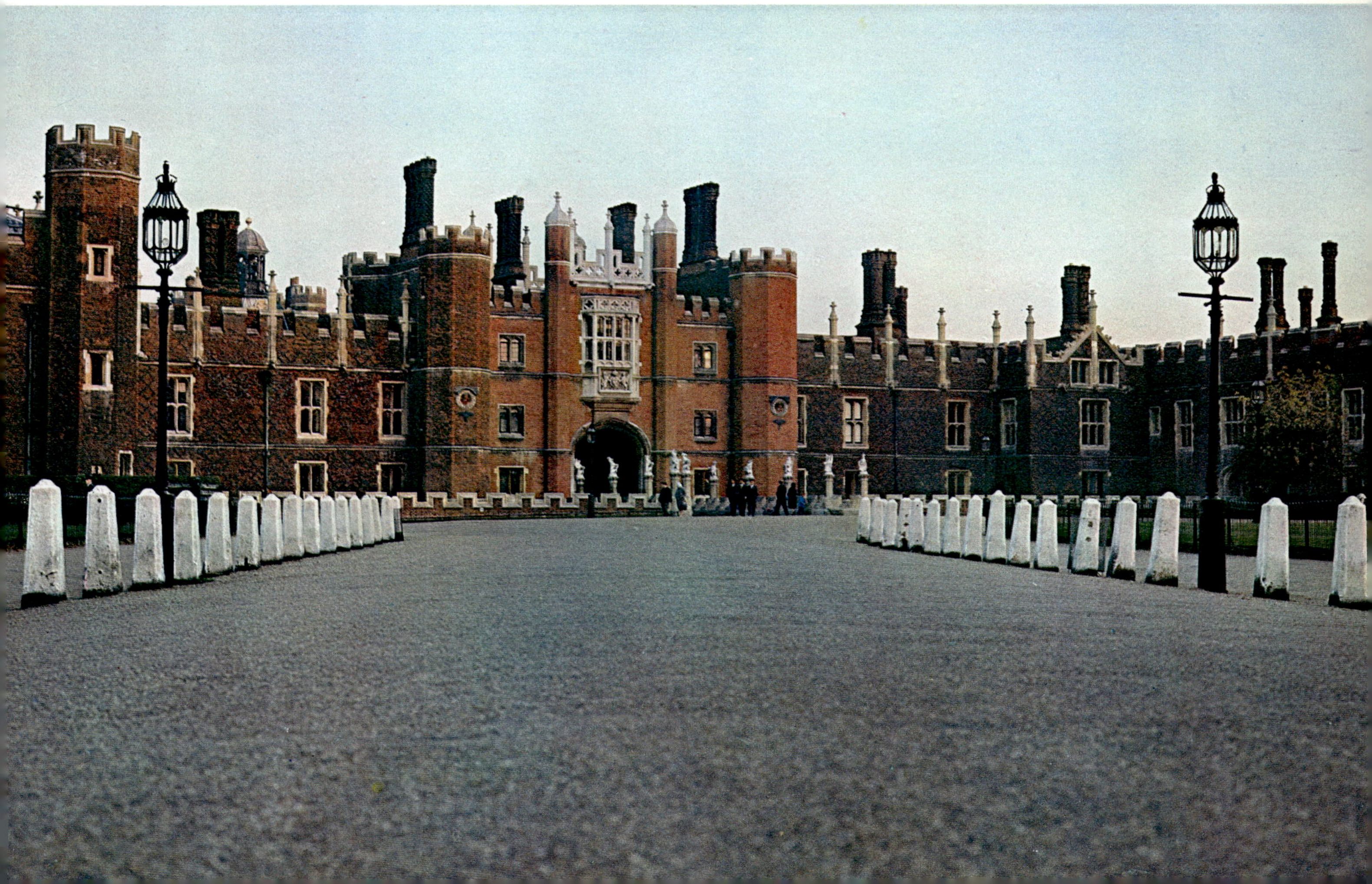

St. Pancras Station: terminus for main railway connections with the Midlands and the North. Designed in the Gothic style by Sir Gilbert Scott

Right: Southwark Cathedral. One of the finest examples of Gothic architecture in London

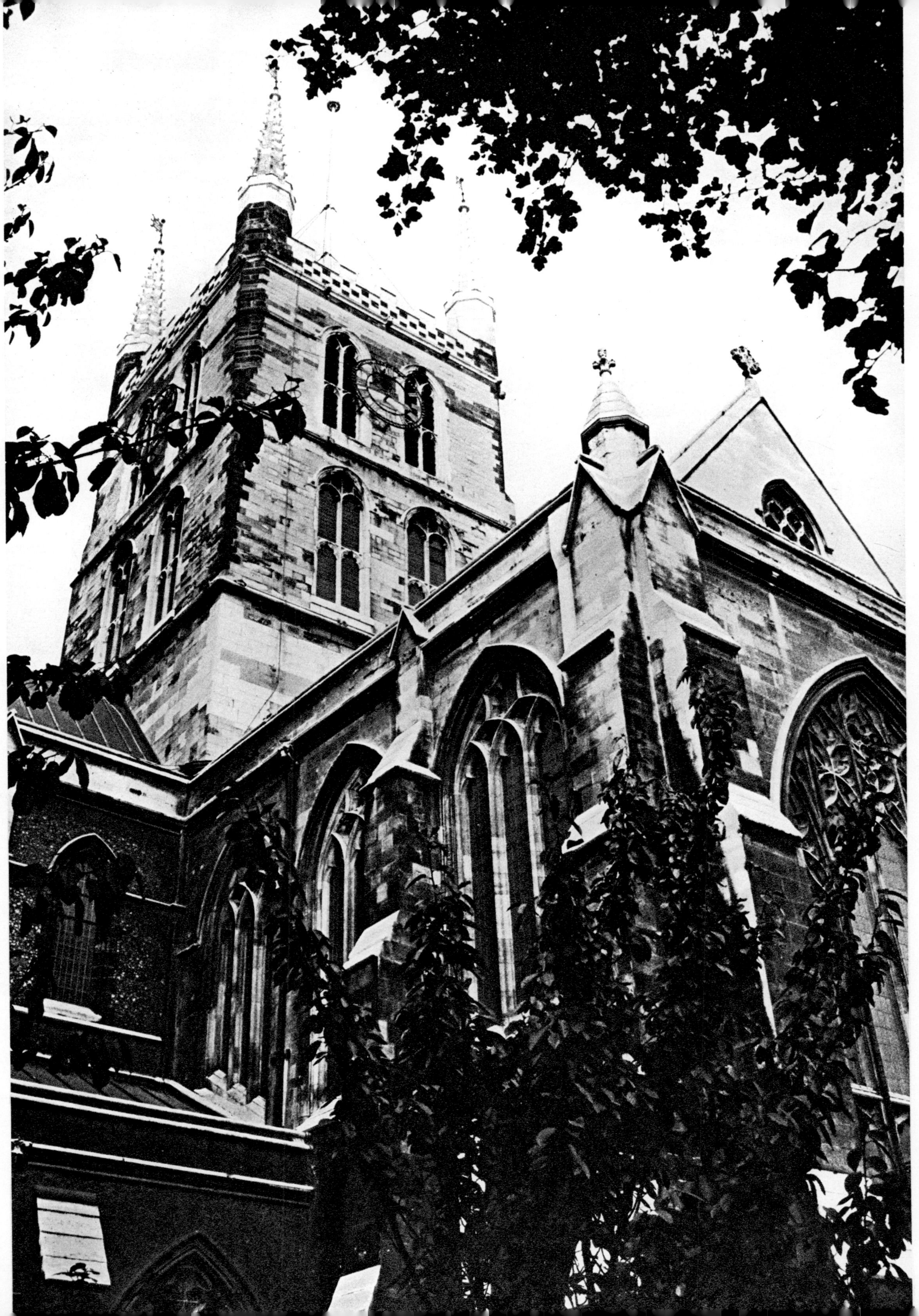

London's youngsters have a wide choice of parks for uninhibited playing – such as conker gathering during the autumn

Holland Park

The Cenotaph, Whitehall

Cleopatra's Needle, Victoria Embankment

The memorial stone to Sir Winston Churchill in Westminster Abbey

Right: the field of remembrance for the dead of two wars, Westminster Abbey

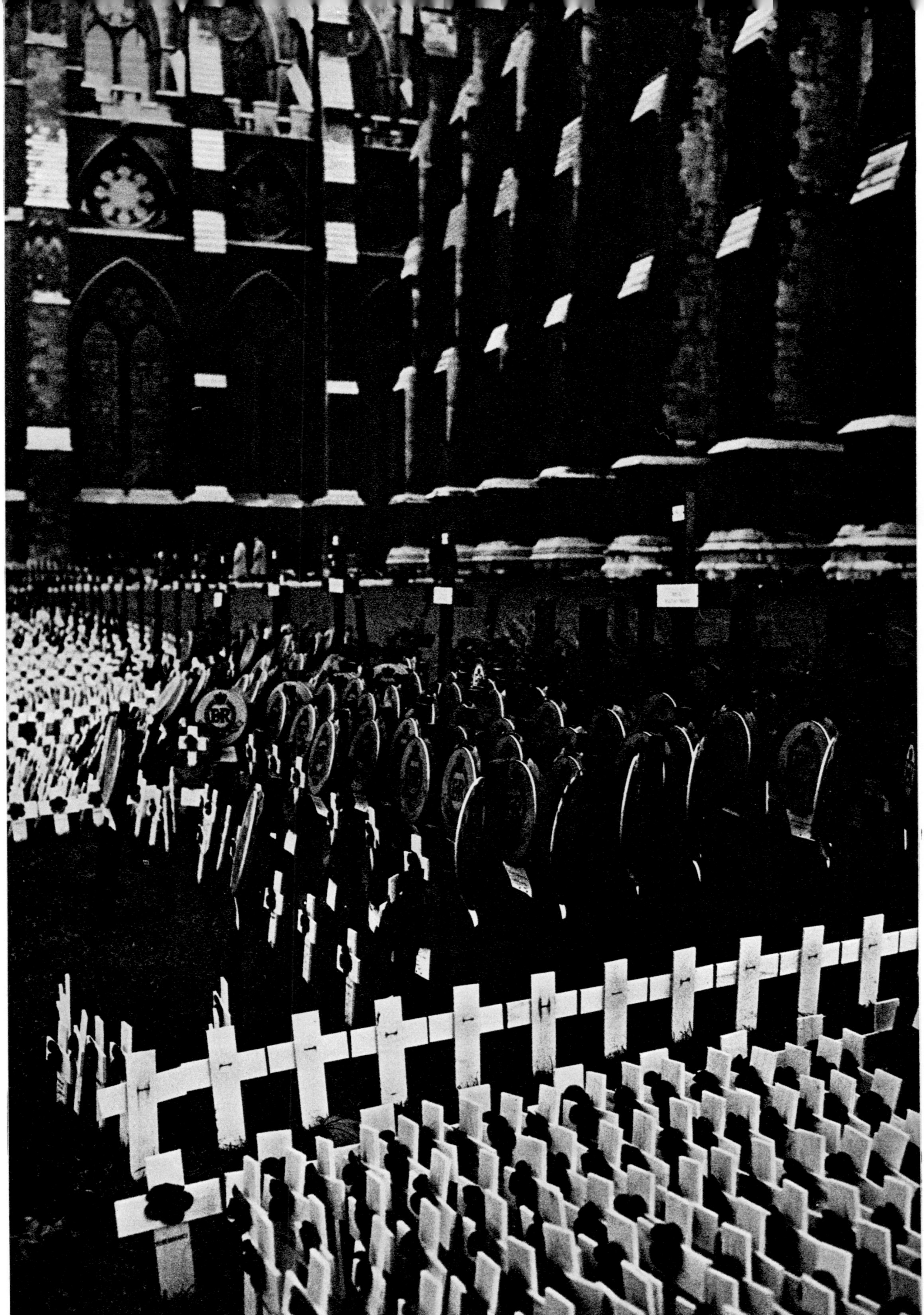

The church of All Hallows by the Tower from where Pepys watched the Great Fire of London. The parent Lamp of Maintenance from which all Toc H lamps are lit is in the sanctuary

Right: the church of St. George-in-the-East by Hawksmoor. Its interior was gutted in 1941, has now been rebuilt within the original shell

CANNON STREET ROAD

London parks can spring surprises. During the summer there is an open-air exhibition of modern sculpture in Battersea Park. Work here is by Edward Paolozzi (*above*) and Barbara Hepworth

169

Brompton Oratory, Knightsbridge

The church of St. Bartholomew the Great, the second oldest church in London (the oldest is the chapel in the White Tower)

The church of St. Mary-le-Bow, Cheapside. Sir Christopher Wren, 1670. Only those born within the sound of Bow bells can properly claim to be true Cockneys

The church of St. George, Hanover Square, early 18th century, popular for fashionable weddings

The Gabo exhibition at the Tate Gallery. The permanent collection here is completely British from the 16th century, otherwise comprehensive and international

In Piccadilly: a building is covered while its stone is cleaned

Victorian London: *Left:* a dolphin coils round the base of a lamp post on the Victoria Embankment. *Below left:* detail of the Albert Memorial. *Below right:* Grecian influence in the friezes on the Royal College of Organists

Sir Joshua Reynolds and Burlington House where the Royal Academy has its galleries

Young, modern artists are shown by small, independent galleries such as the Kasmin Gallery (*above*) and the Robert Fraser Gallery (*right*)

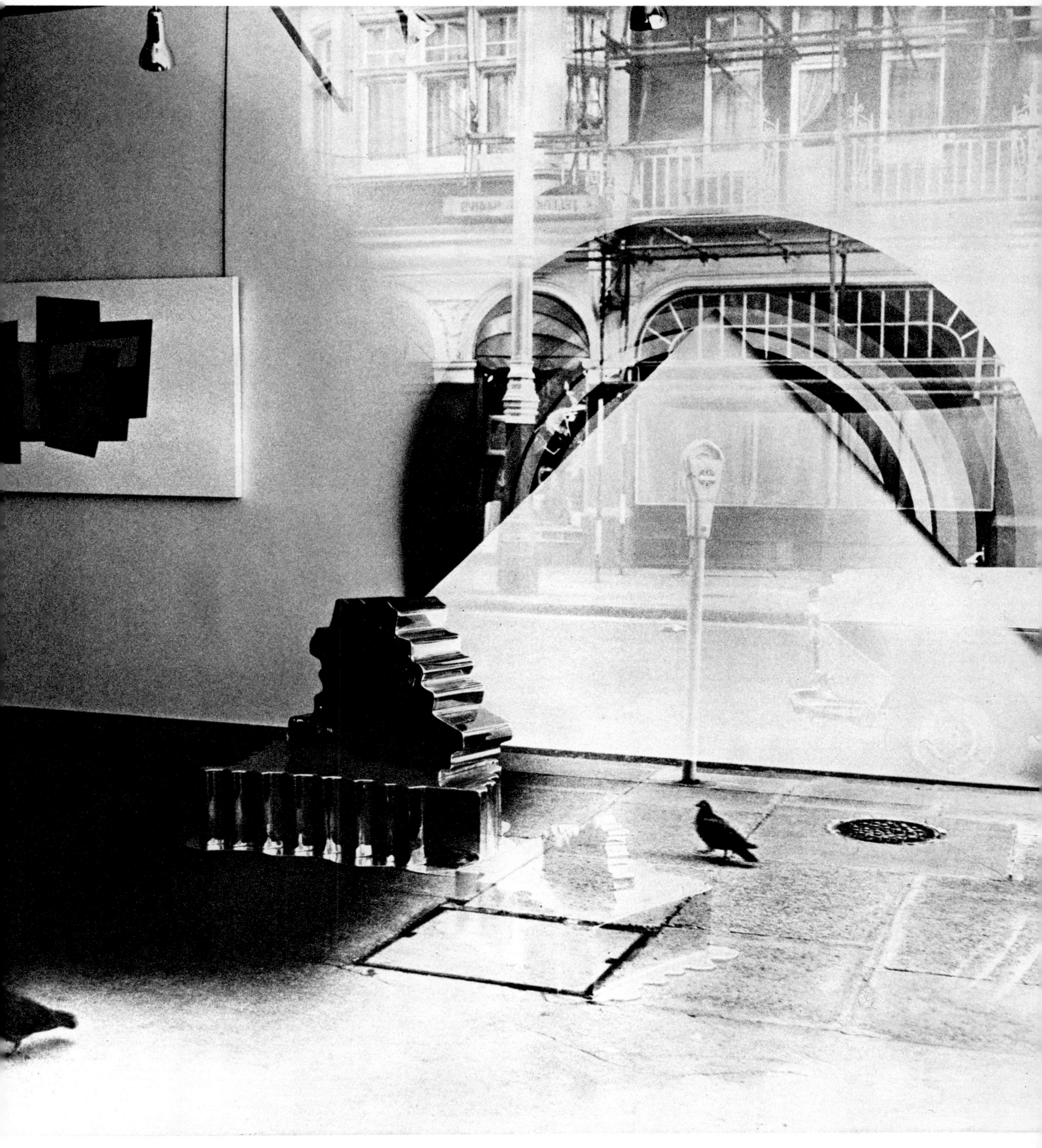

Contrasts in art. The National Gallery in Trafalgar Square (*top*) houses the national collection representing western European art. Outside the gallery a casual pavement artist produces instant portraits

London has become a centre for international, experimental artists. Here Yoko Ono (*centre*) presents a demonstration she calls Handkerchief Piece

The British Museum, Bloomsbury, unrivalled for the scope and richness of its collections. Among the most popular exhibits are (*right*) the mummies and coffins in the Egyptian rooms

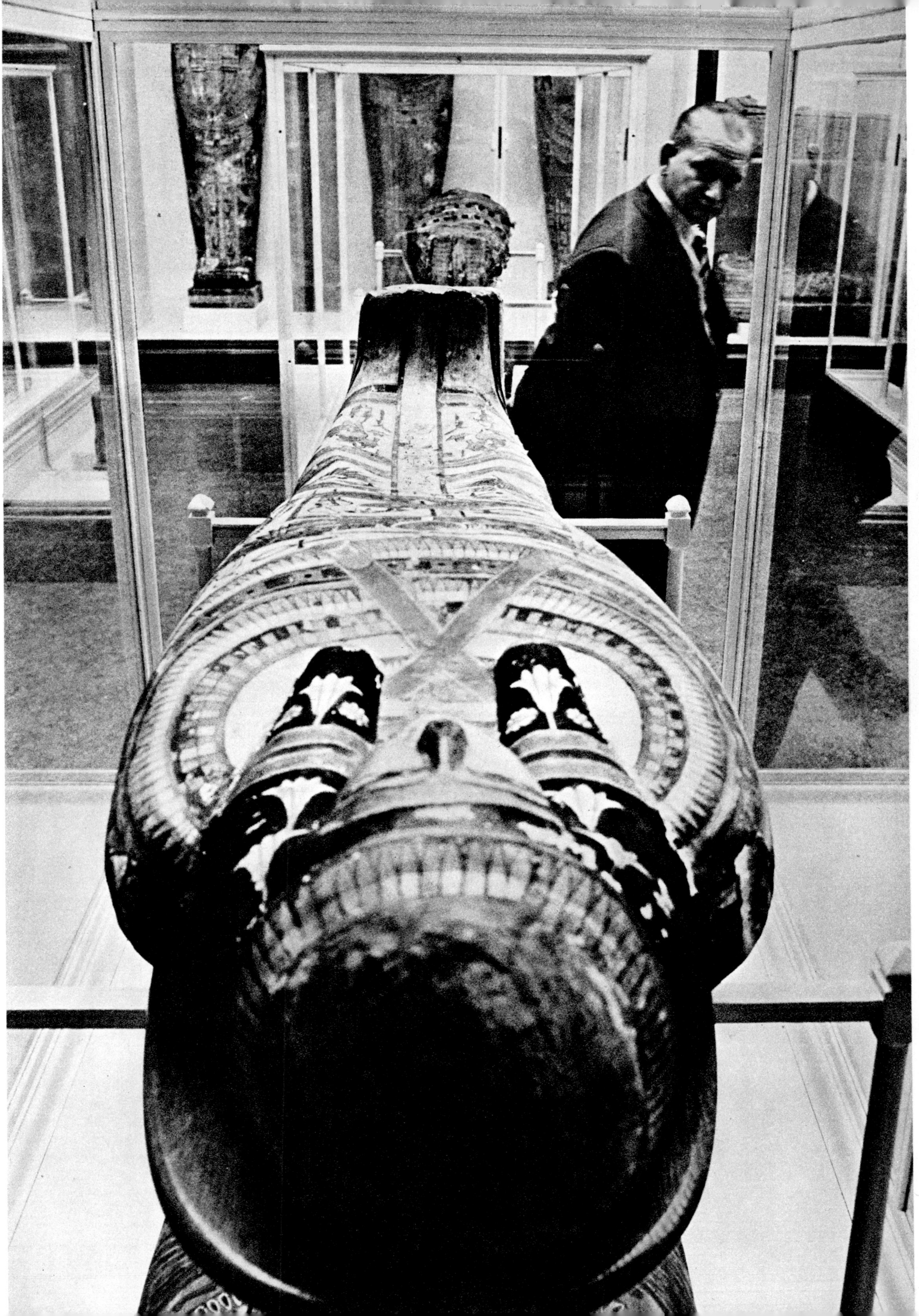

The Victoria and Albert Museum, South Kensington, contains one of the finest collections of applied art in the world. The Raphael cartoons (*above*) hang here and there is a fine collection of costumes, also of furniture. The panelled room (*right*) dates from 1730, is from Hatton Garden, Holborn

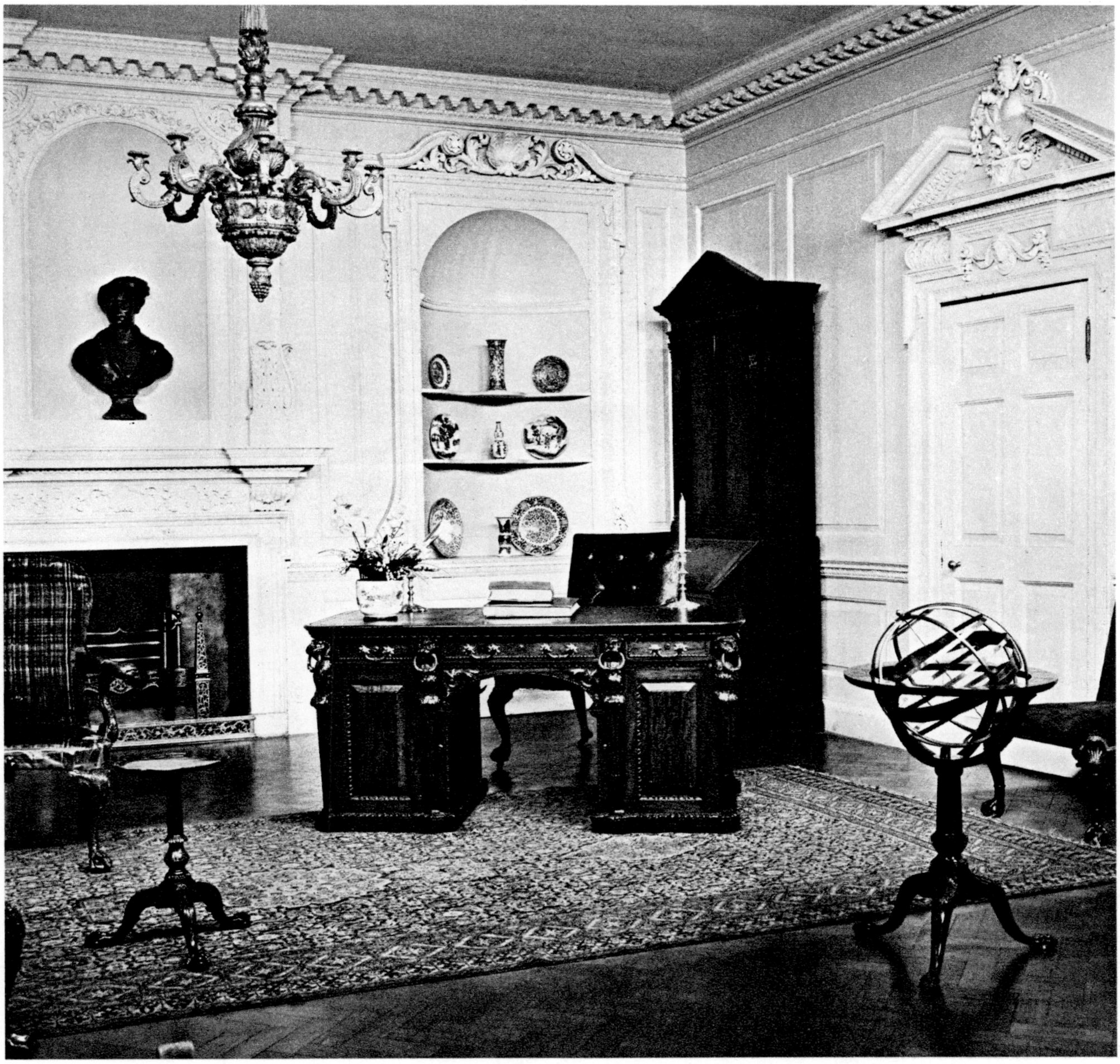

The statue of Dr. Johnson outside the choir of St. Clement Danes in the Strand. This church has a particularly tuneful peal of bells commemorated in the nursery rhyme: "Oranges and lemons say the bells of St. Clement's"

Right: the church of St. Bride, just off Fleet Street considered to be one of the finest examples of Wren's work

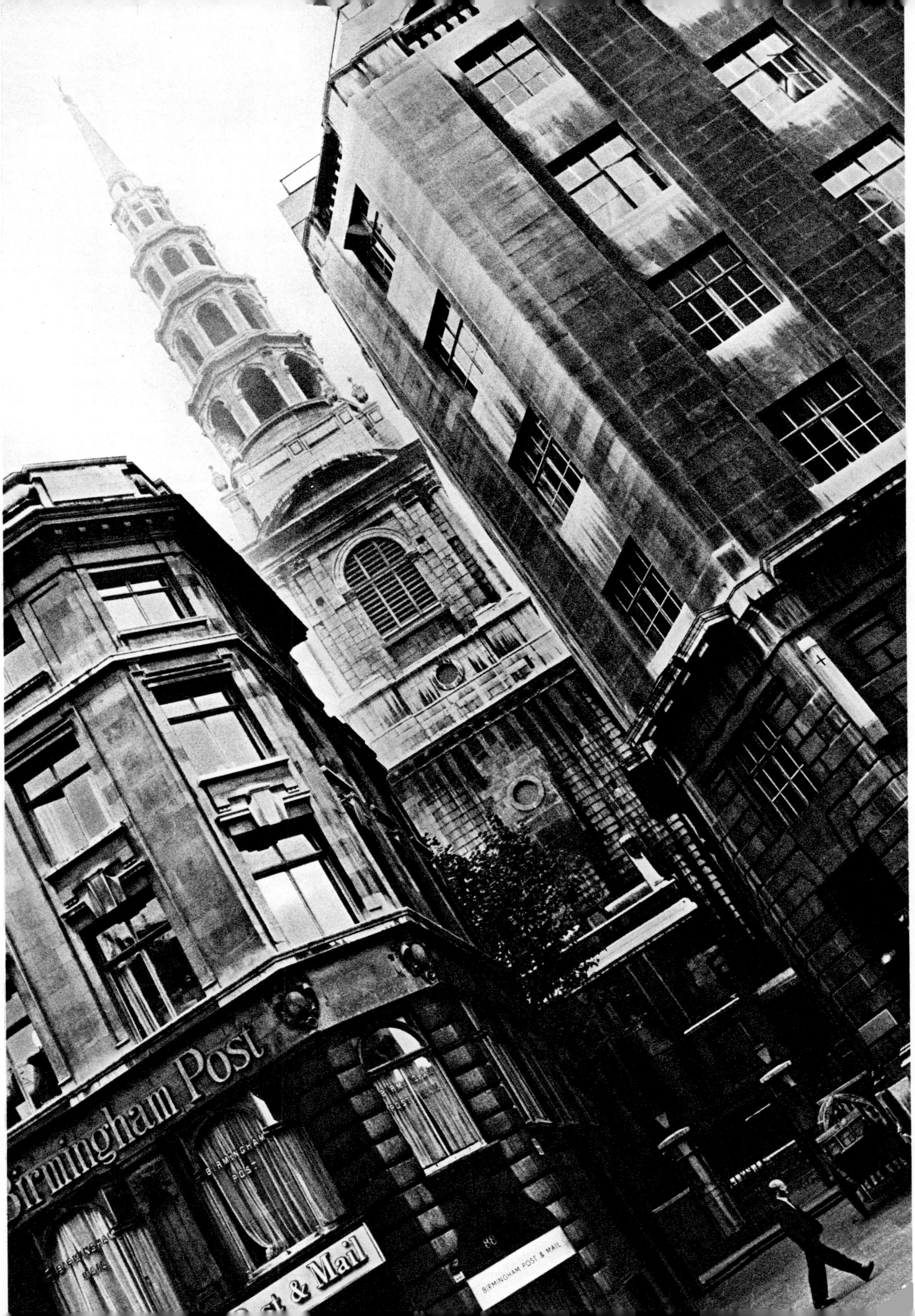
Birmingham Post
BIRMINGHAM POST
BIRMINGHAM POST & MAIL

Seen from the south bank of the Thames, Sir Gilbert Scott's Houses of Parliament revealing the basic symmetry of the river front

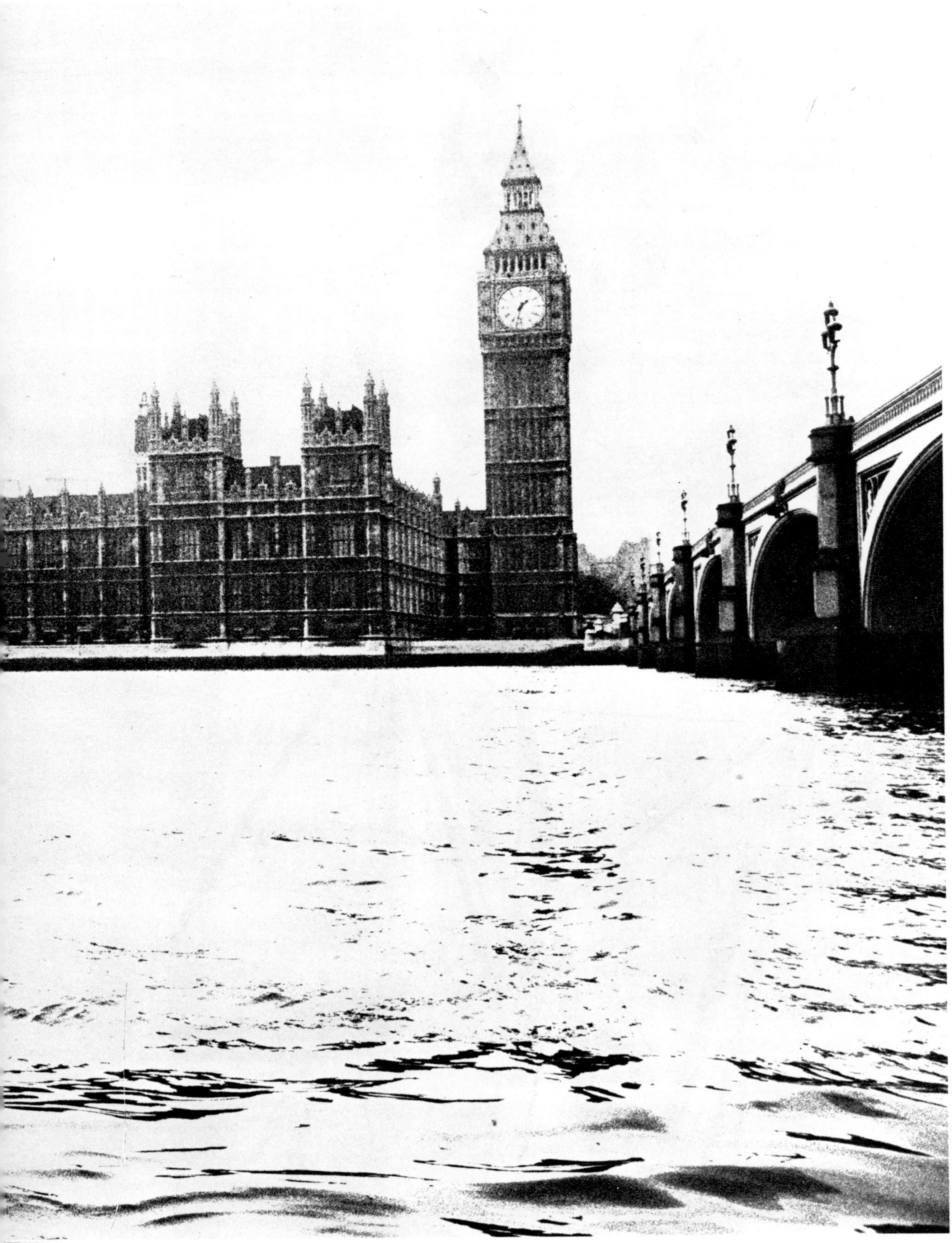

190

The Zoological Gardens are currently undergoing complete re-formation giving modern architects a chance to experiment and to give the animals the best conditions. The Aviary (*opposite*) was designed by Lord Snowdon; the giant panda Chi-Chi is the most valuable possession

In Madame Tussaud's waxwork exhibition. There are more than 360 models, all made on the premises. The Chamber of Horrors has 73 chilling exhibits including this group of celebrated contemporary murderers and the famous Dr. Crippen (*right*)

193

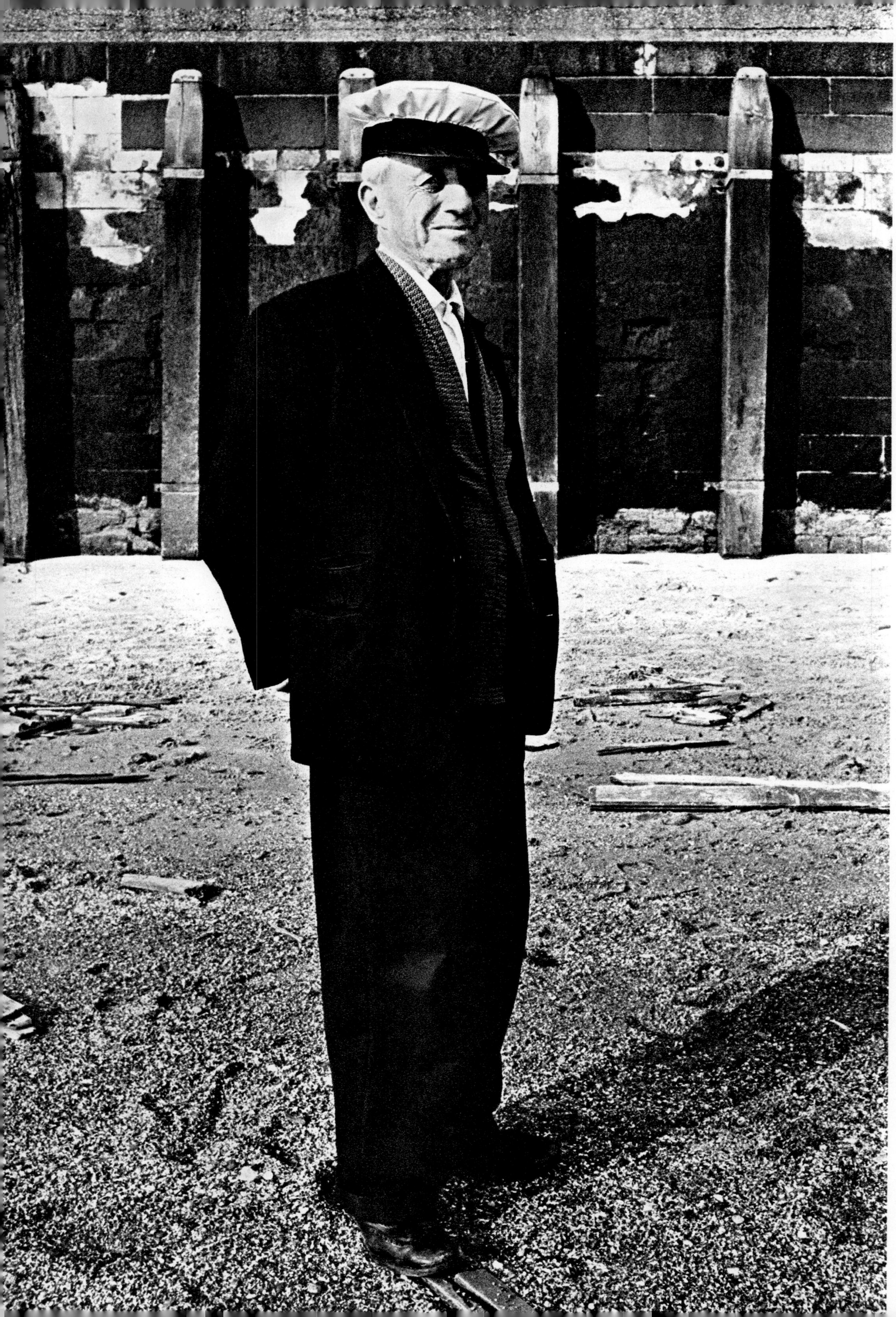

The Tower of London and its Traitors' Gate through which prisoners were brought by water. It is now closed and fronted by a stretch of sand accessible by steps lowered by an attendant (*left*) at low tide

St. James's Palace, known affectionately by guardsmen as Jimmy's, is an oddly-shaped redbrick building, the gatehouse of which faces St. James's Street. The Lord Chamberlain has his offices here

Yeoman Warder, Tower of London

Hampton Court Palace on the Thames fifteen miles from central London was built as a private residence by Cardinal Wolsey in 1514 but relinquished to Henry VIII. Looking through the Base Court to Ann Boleyn's Gatehouse

St. Martin in the Fields, Trafalgar Square, generally regarded as the best work of James Gibbs. It was built between 1721 and 1726

Kenwood, a house at Hampstead reconstructed in 1767 by Robert Adam and containing a fine collection of pictures and furniture. The painting is of Mary, Countess Howe by Gainsborough. Photographed by courtesy of the Iveagh Bequest

Kenwood: the lake in the 200 acre grounds

Kenwood: the house seen from the lake

Goldfish browse beneath the waterlily pads of a pond at Kew Gardens, and (*below*) a watchful black cat rests on a tombstone at Kensal Green Cemetery

Kew Gardens: the palm house and setting sun

At Kew Gardens, 288 acres with more than 25,000 varieties of plants

The rotunda, Kew Gardens

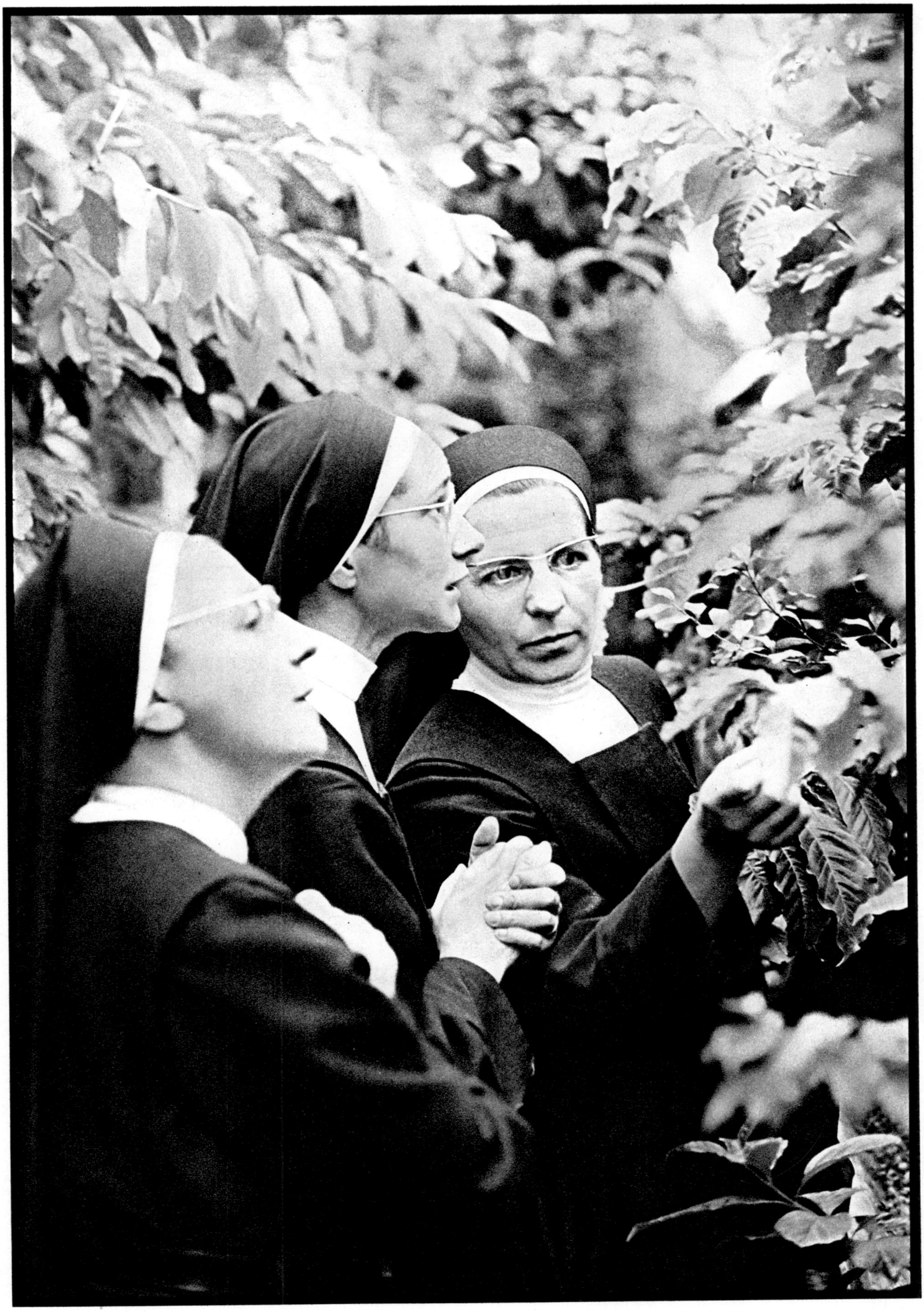

Shows, exhibitions and displays of all kinds fall thickly during the year. Cruft's, the annual dog show held at Olympia is now an important event in the social calendar

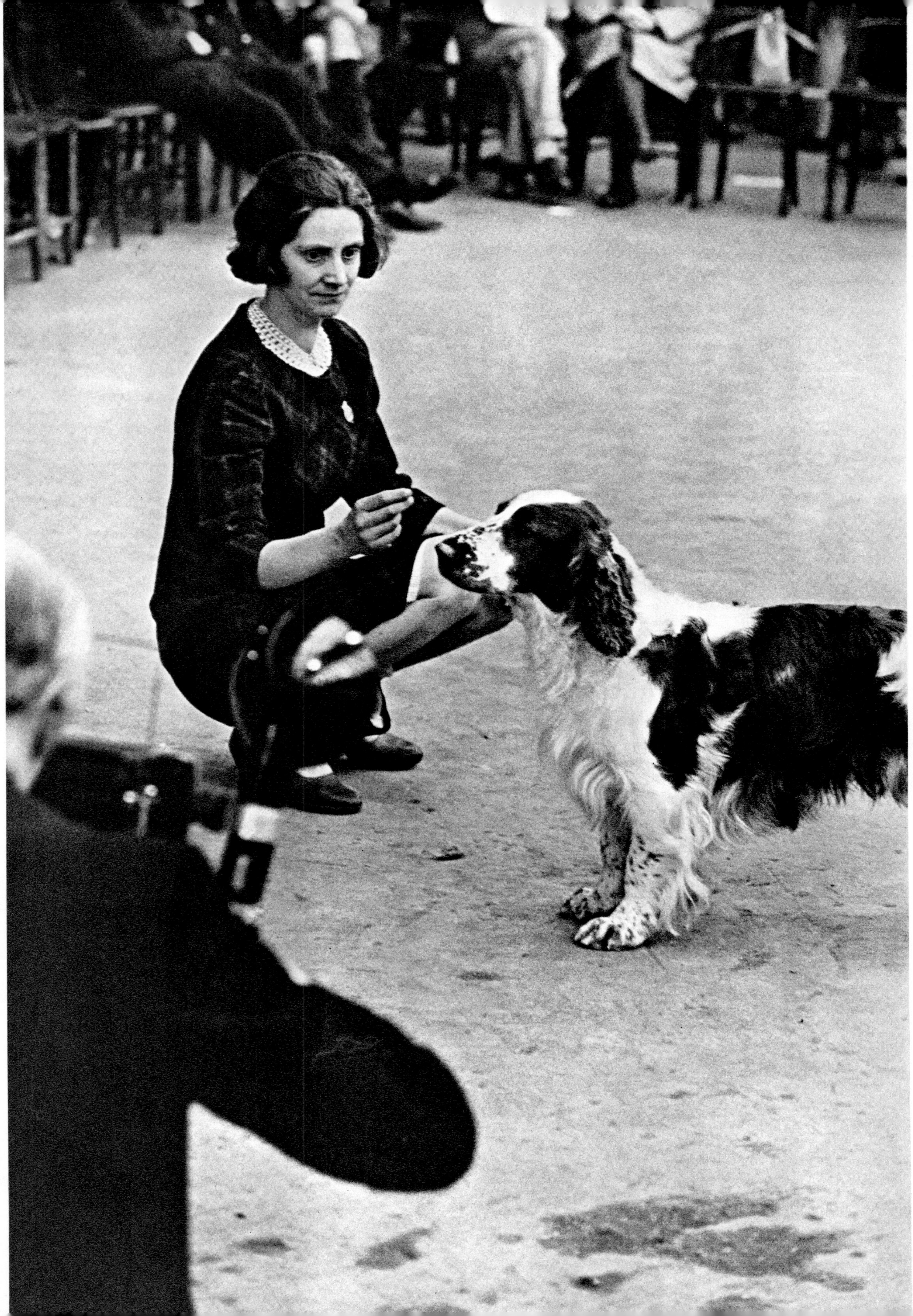

Policeman in the Mall, ceremonial way from Buckingham Palace; trading vehicles are not allowed, nor are taxis allowed to ply for hire, as in the royal parks

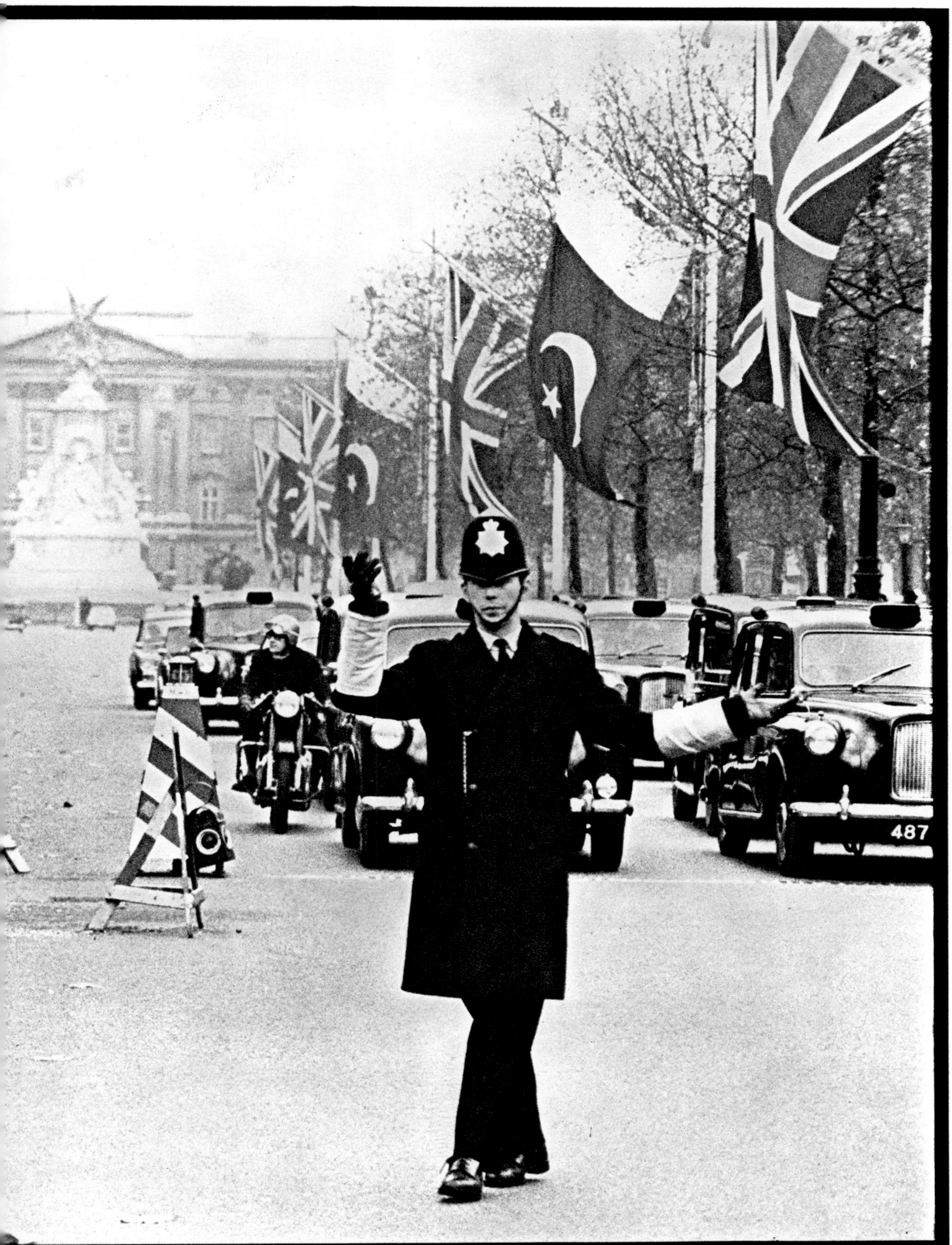
487

Centre Court, Wimbledon tennis tournament, a world-famous summer event

Out at Greenwich the last of the sailing clippers, the **Cutty Sark**, rests in dry dock

Reconstructed pub on Hampstead Heath, Jack Straw's Castle

From the roof of the Hilton Hotel, Park Lane, the solid block of well-wooded countryside is Hyde Park. The Serpentine glimmers in the distance, to the left Knightsbridge and beyond, Kensington

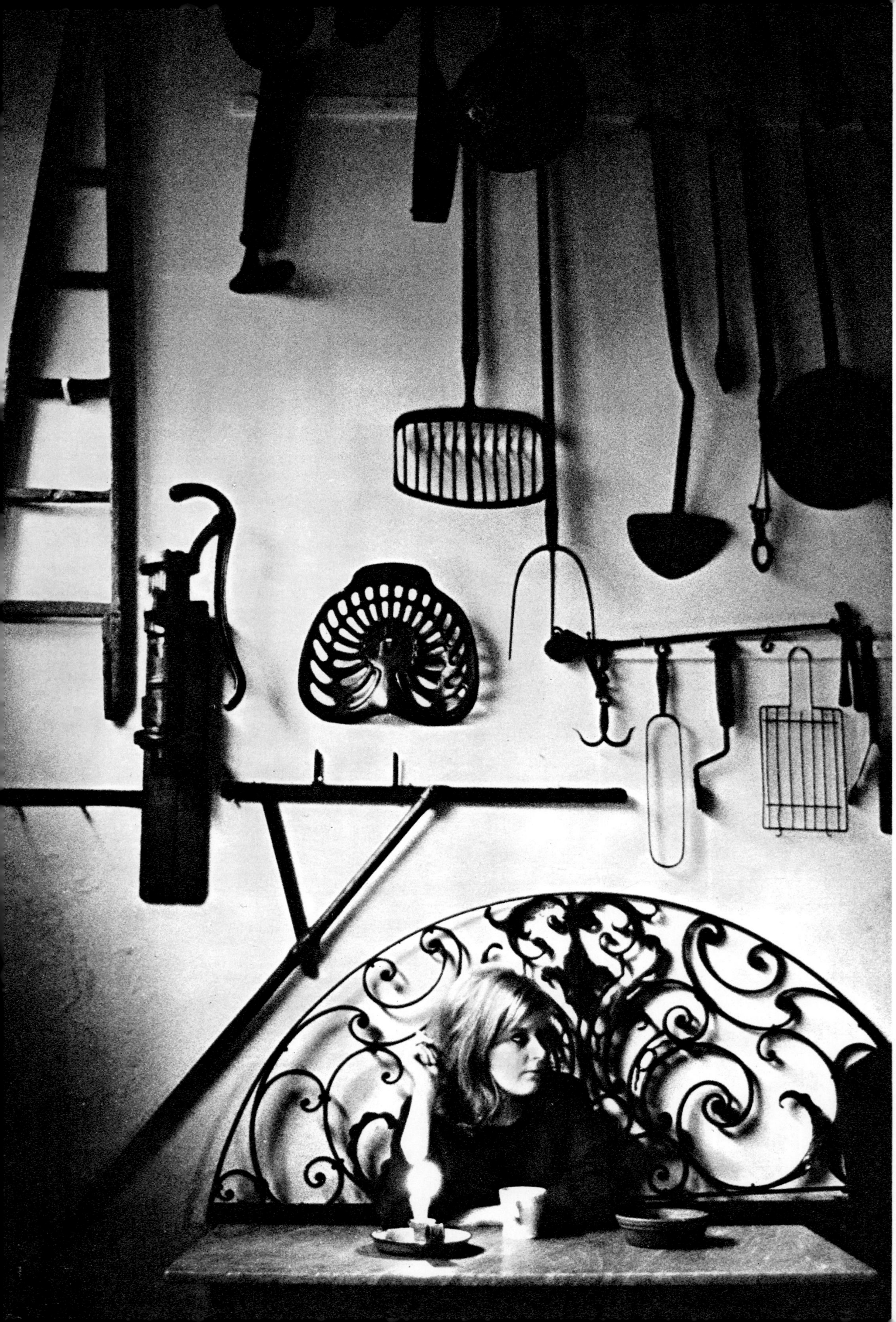

Contrasts for the afternoon: sitting in a coffee bar, just chatting (*left*) or seeking unexpected views of familiar places, such as St. Paul's Cathedral framed by riverside warehouses

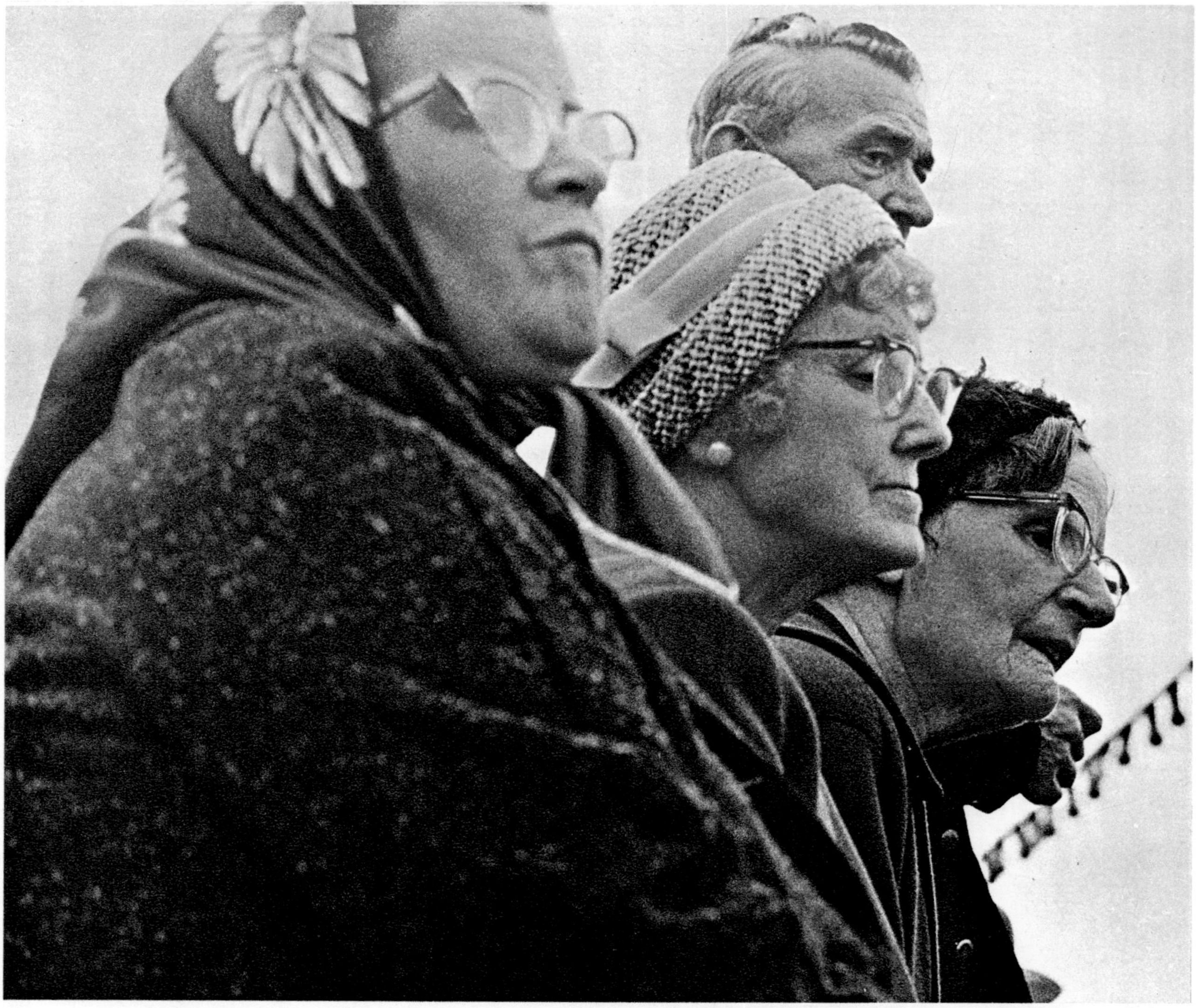

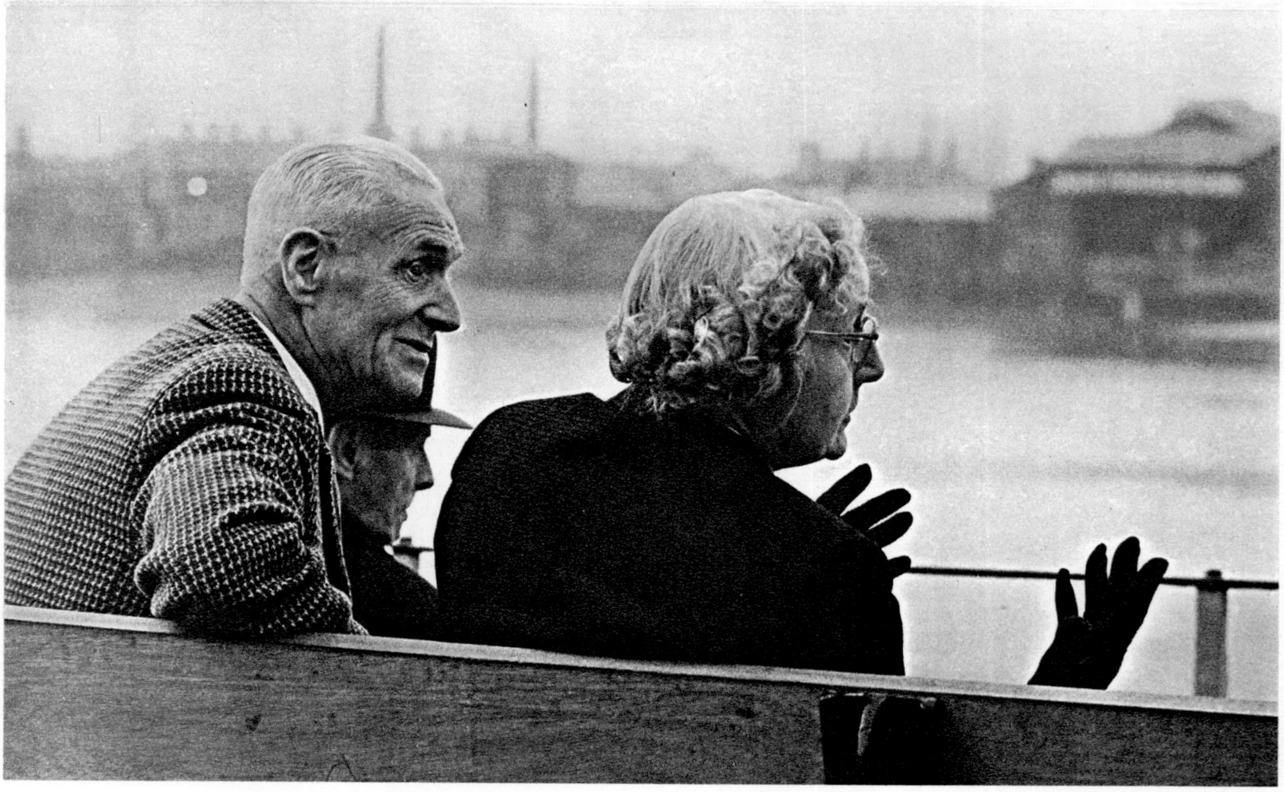

Sunday afternoon at Greenwich; sitting by the river

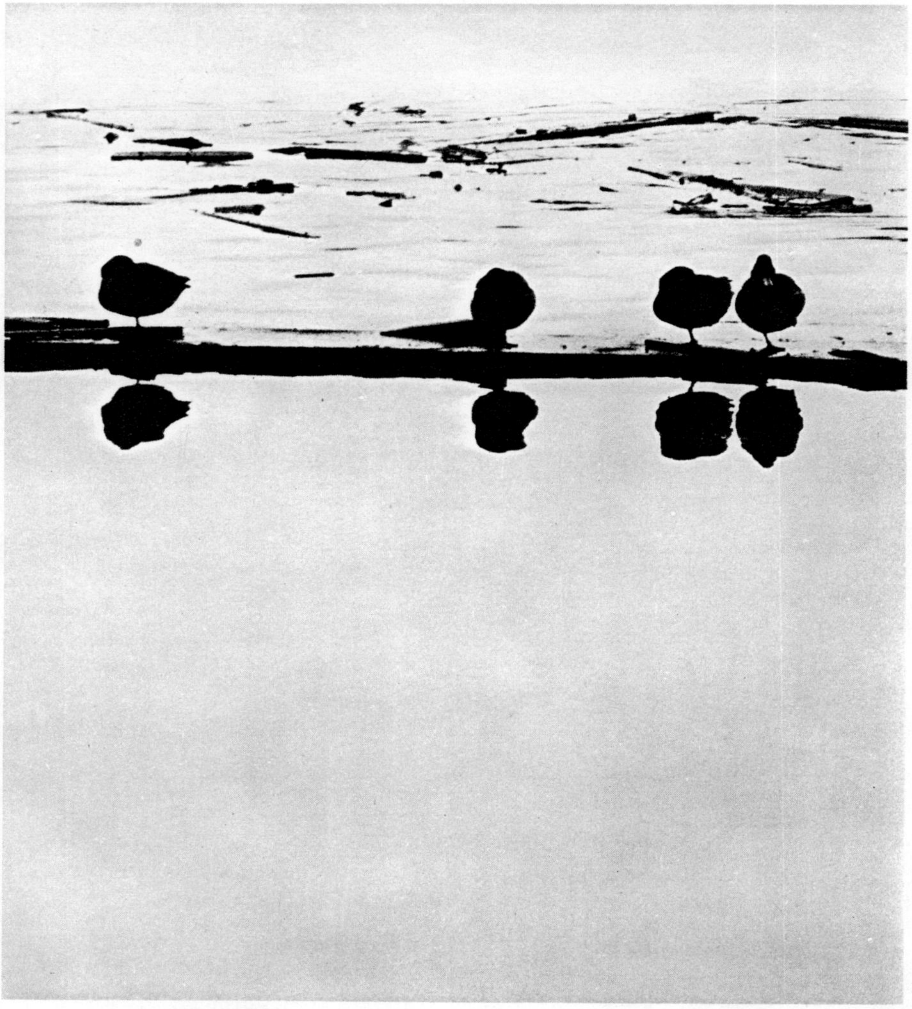

London at Leisure

There are always pockets of peace in the busiest of cities. London is no exception. Peace can mean a solitary walk in a deserted park, or Trafalgar Square with just the pigeons. There are gardens, lakes, quiet alleys, little pubs and secluded squares; all areas of calm slotted into the varied fabric of the city

Flying kites and walking dogs in Regent's Park

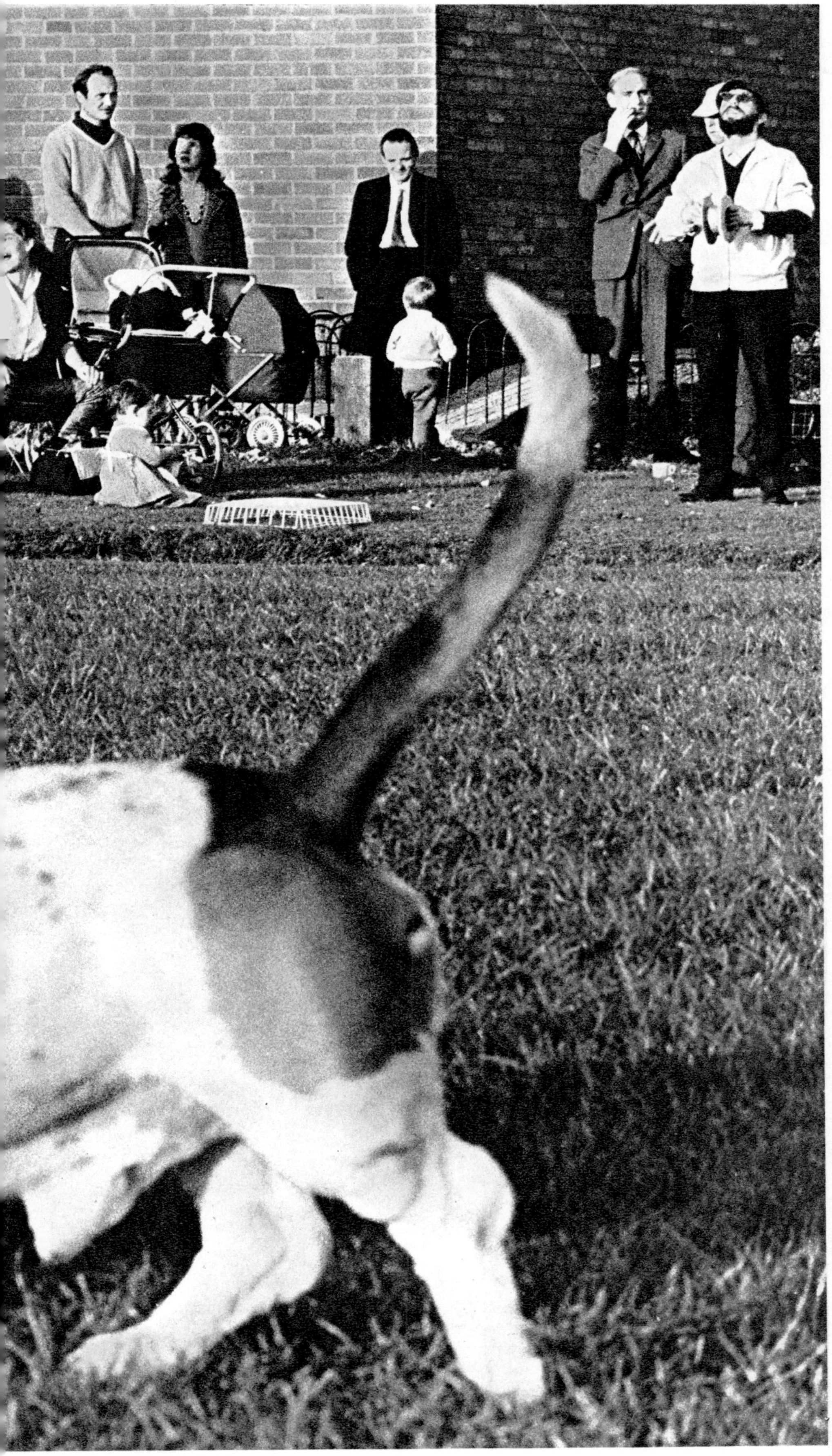

Lincoln's Inn Fields: the W. H. Smith memorial

The Duke of York's column, Waterloo Place. The steps lead down to the Mall

In Shepherd Market, a village within the tall hotels and apartments of Mayfair, there are a number of small antique shops, such as this one with its owner standing outside

Peter Pan's statue, Kensington Gardens. The boy who never grew up, created by J. M. Barrie in his play, annually revived as a Christmas entertainment for children

227

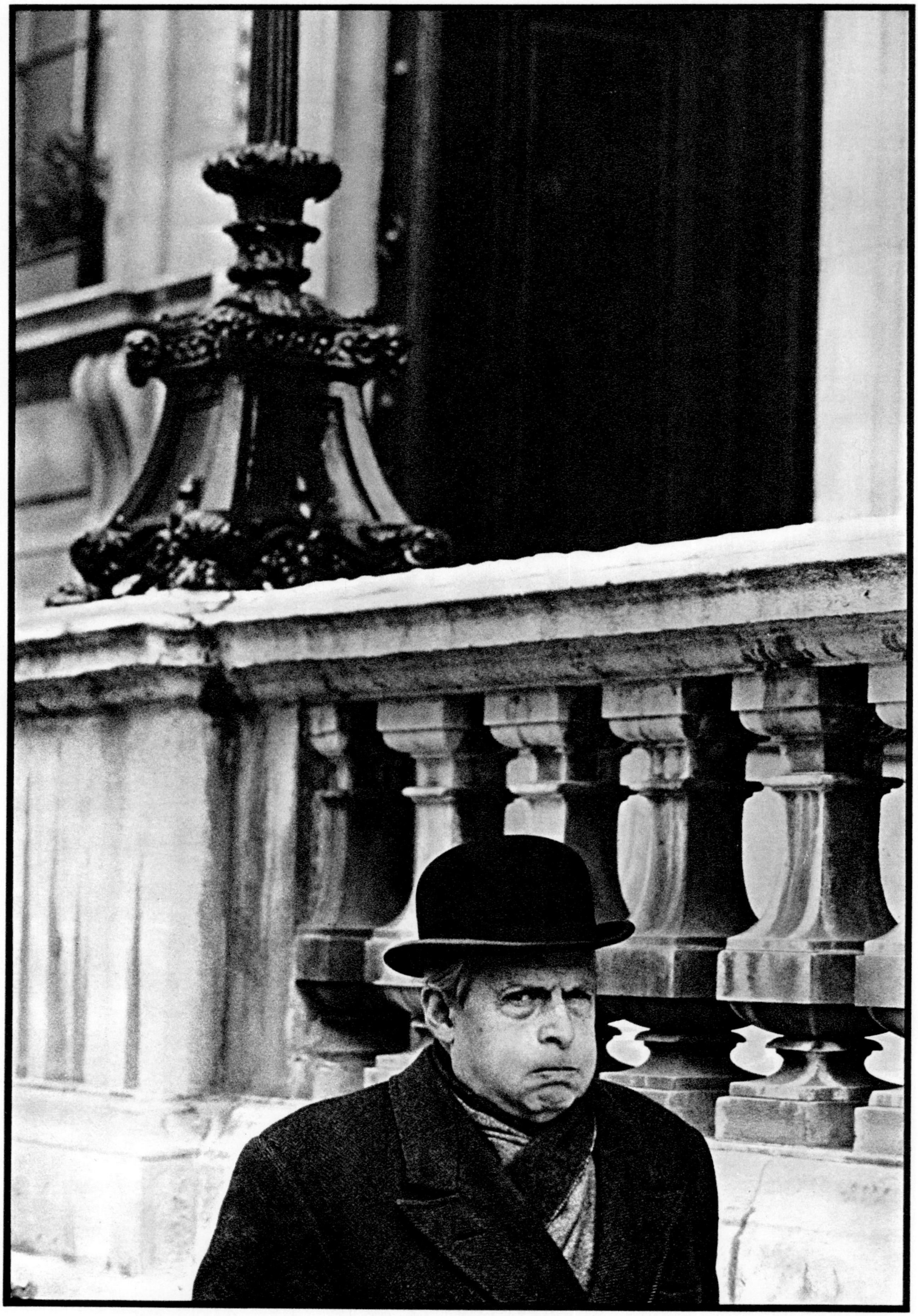

Boodle's Club, St. James's Street. Through the window, a member reads a newspaper. *Left:* the Reform Club, Pall Mall

The Serpentine, Hyde Park: for lazy afternoon boating. In the background, the London Hilton

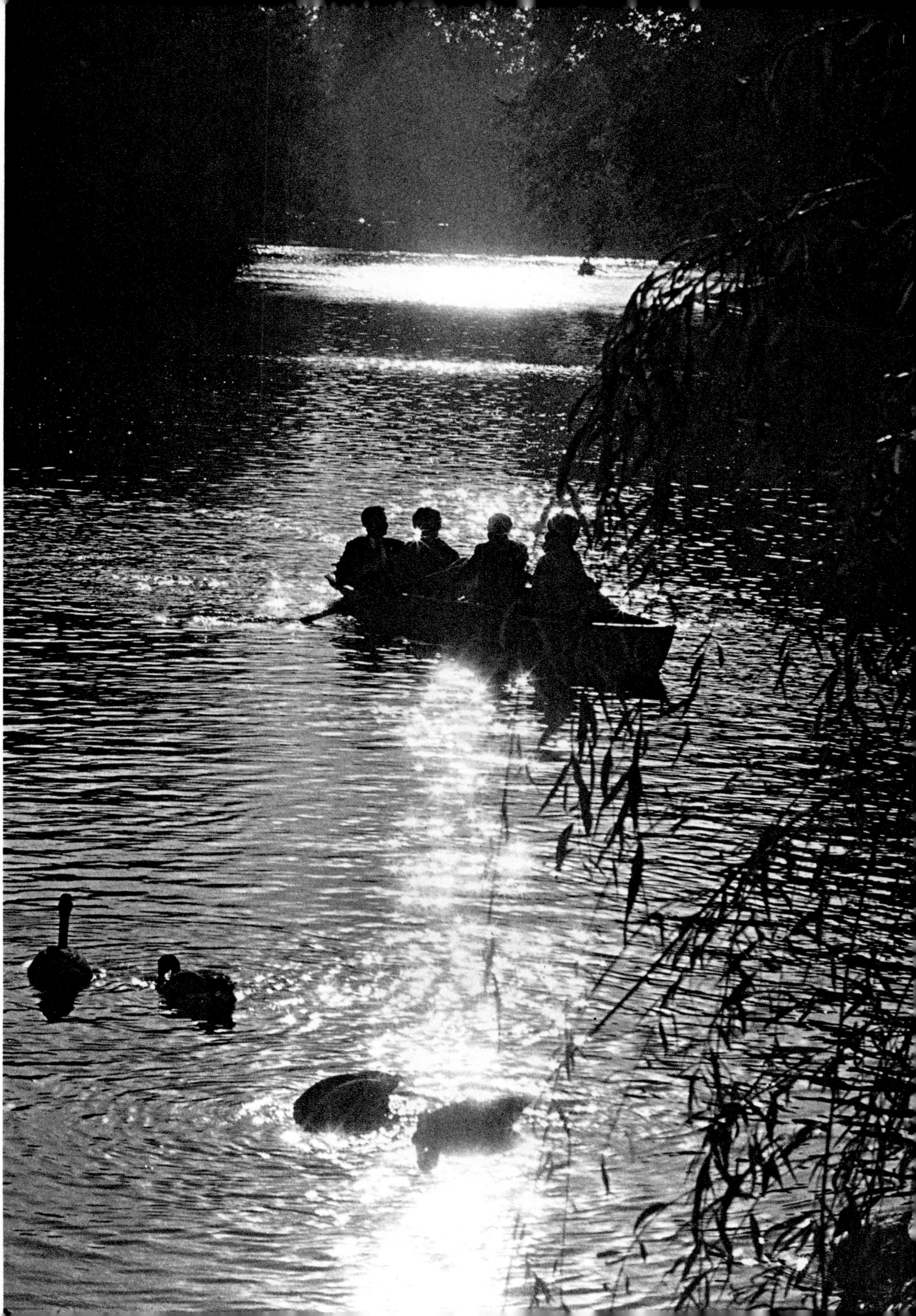

The Albert Memorial, just inside Hyde Park off Kensington Gore, national monument to Queen Victoria's consort

Cable Street in London's east end. Now gradually being demolished, once a notorious area

233

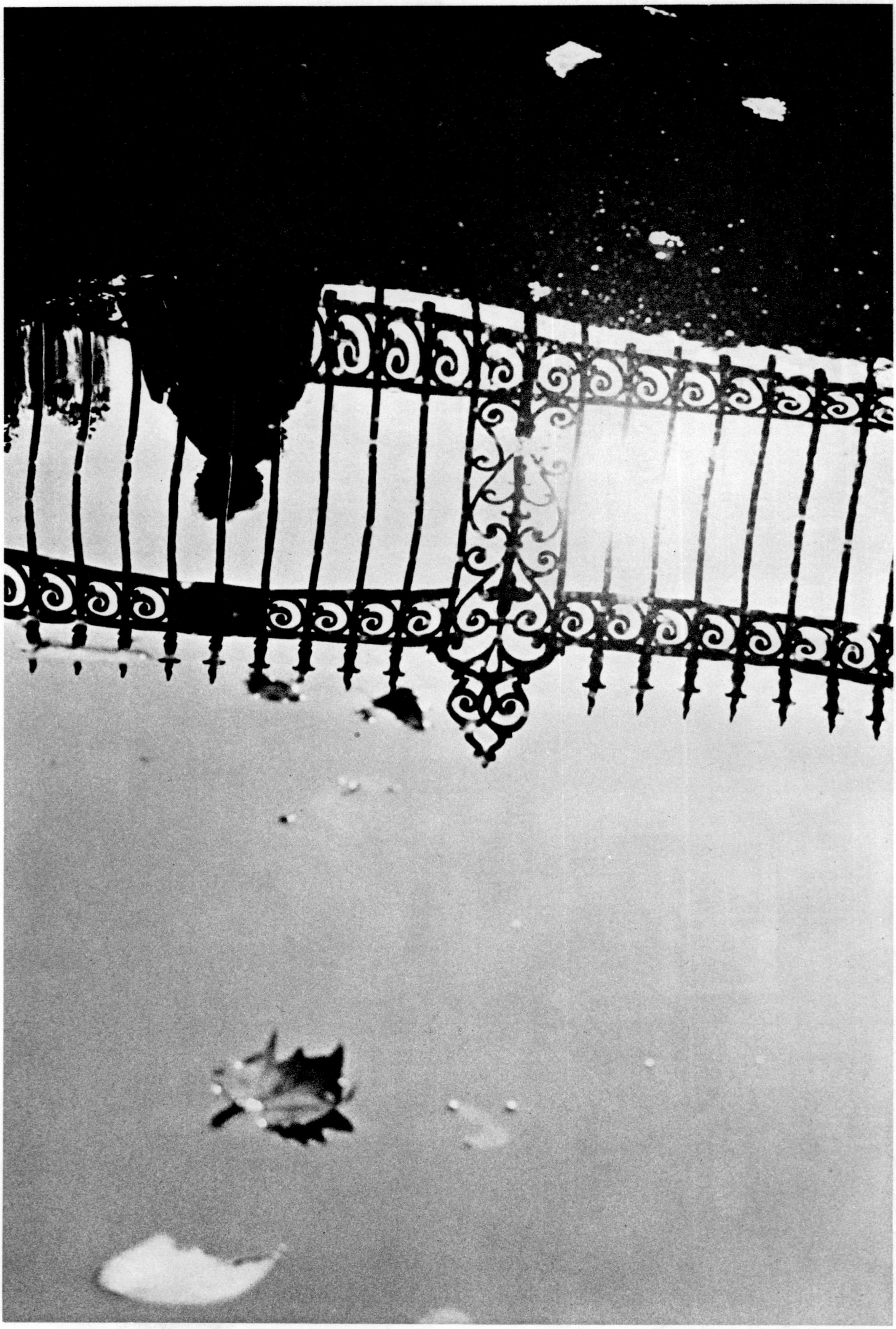

Pause for conversation during leaf-sweeping along Kensington Palace Gardens

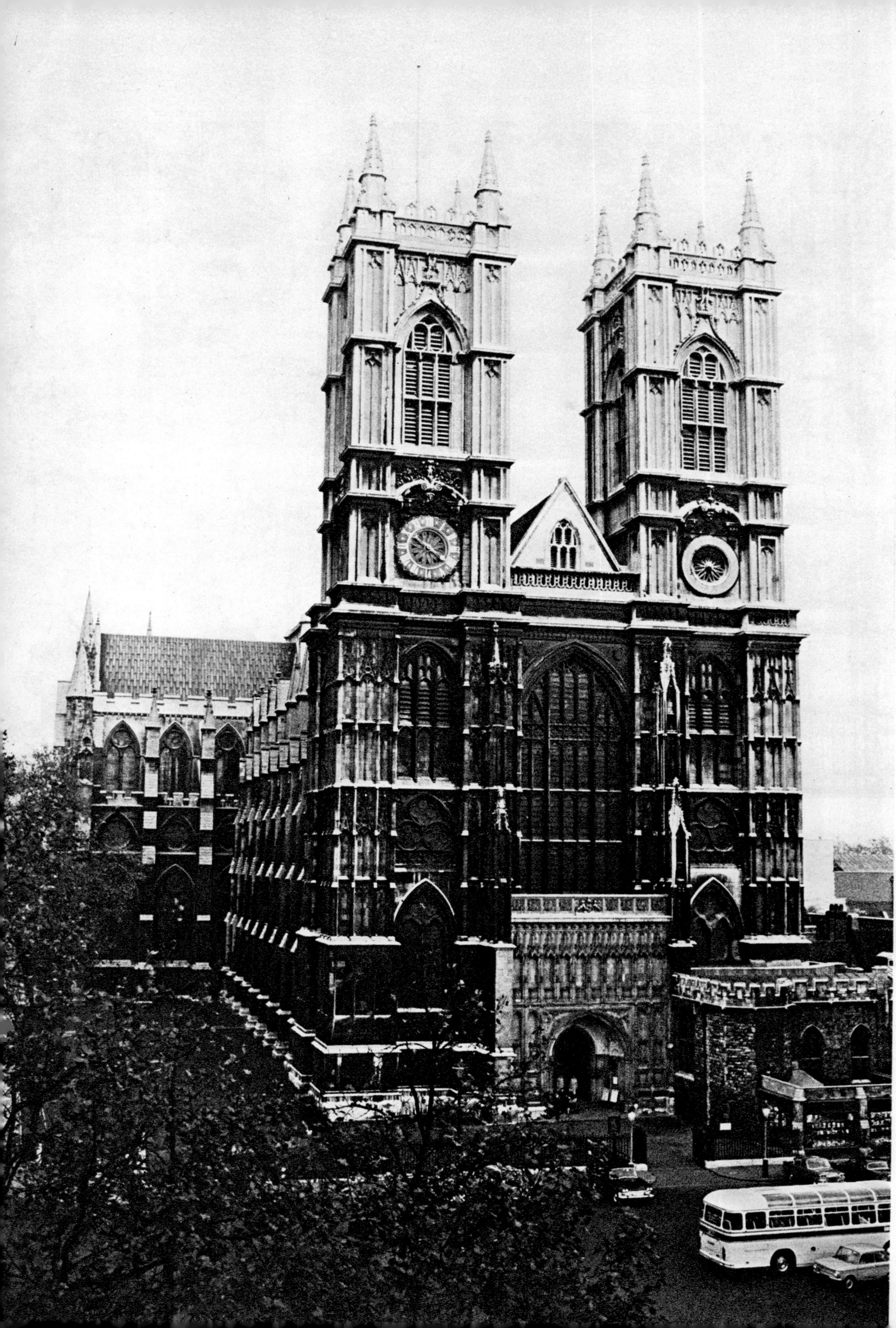

Westminster Abbey: the Great Cloister (earliest parts date from 1250) seen through the glass panels of a door from the nave

Opposite: the west front of the Abbey

Westminster Abbey: detail of the choir screen

Westminster Abbey: the Nave, showing choir screen, and (*below*) one of the Abbey's many tombs, this one commemorating Thomas Owen, a Judge of the Common Pleas under Elizabeth I. The alabaster figure is painted and gilded

The Tower of London: fortress, prison, garrison, now a museum and showplace. Armour, instruments of torture, the Crown Jewels are displayed

The Royal Festival Hall, and boating on the Thames

St. James's Palace

The Prospect of Whitby, well-known riverside pub in the East End

The Salisbury, St. Martin's Lane. In the middle of theatreland, supreme example of gilt, plush, carved looking-glass and Edwardian splendour

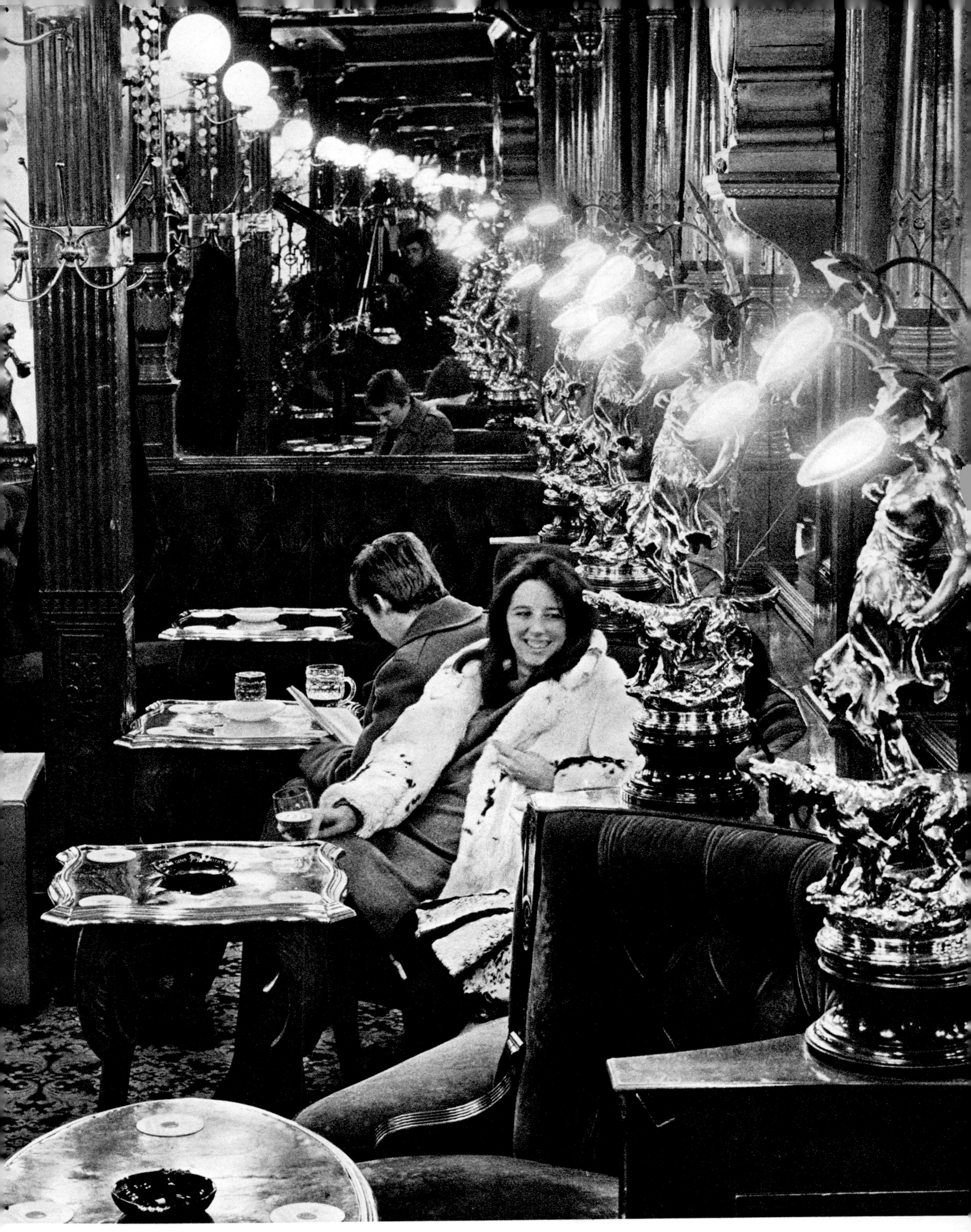

The Doves Inn, Upper Mall, Hammersmith. Overlooks the river, has pleasant beamed bars, small terrace

Right: Kensington Gardens; the bandstand

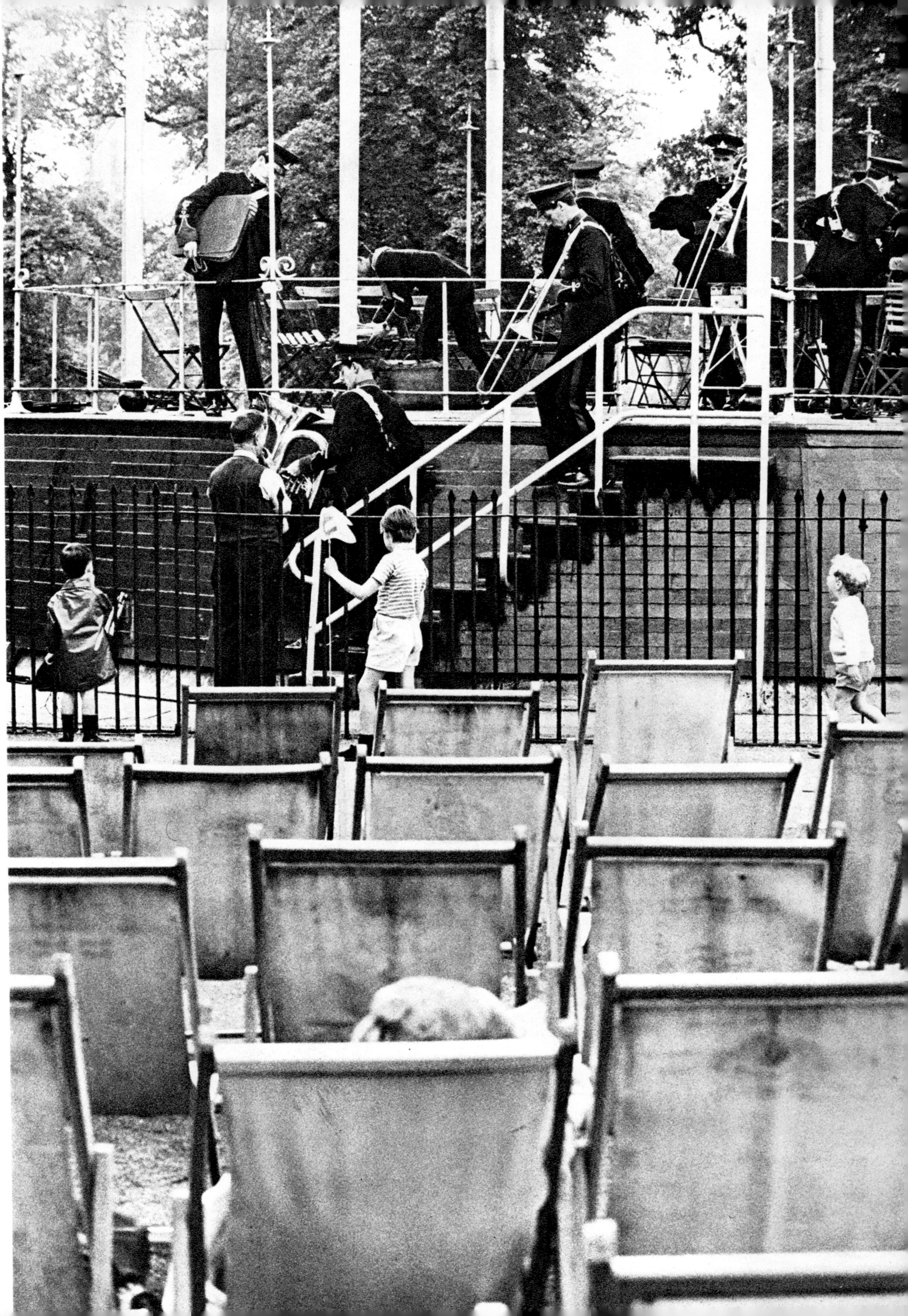

The Cheshire Cheese, one of the more famous pubs off Fleet Street. Associations with Dr. Johnson, Boswell, Goldsmith

Right: The George Inn, Southwark. Last remaining galleried inn in the London area. Use is made of the galleries to perform plays

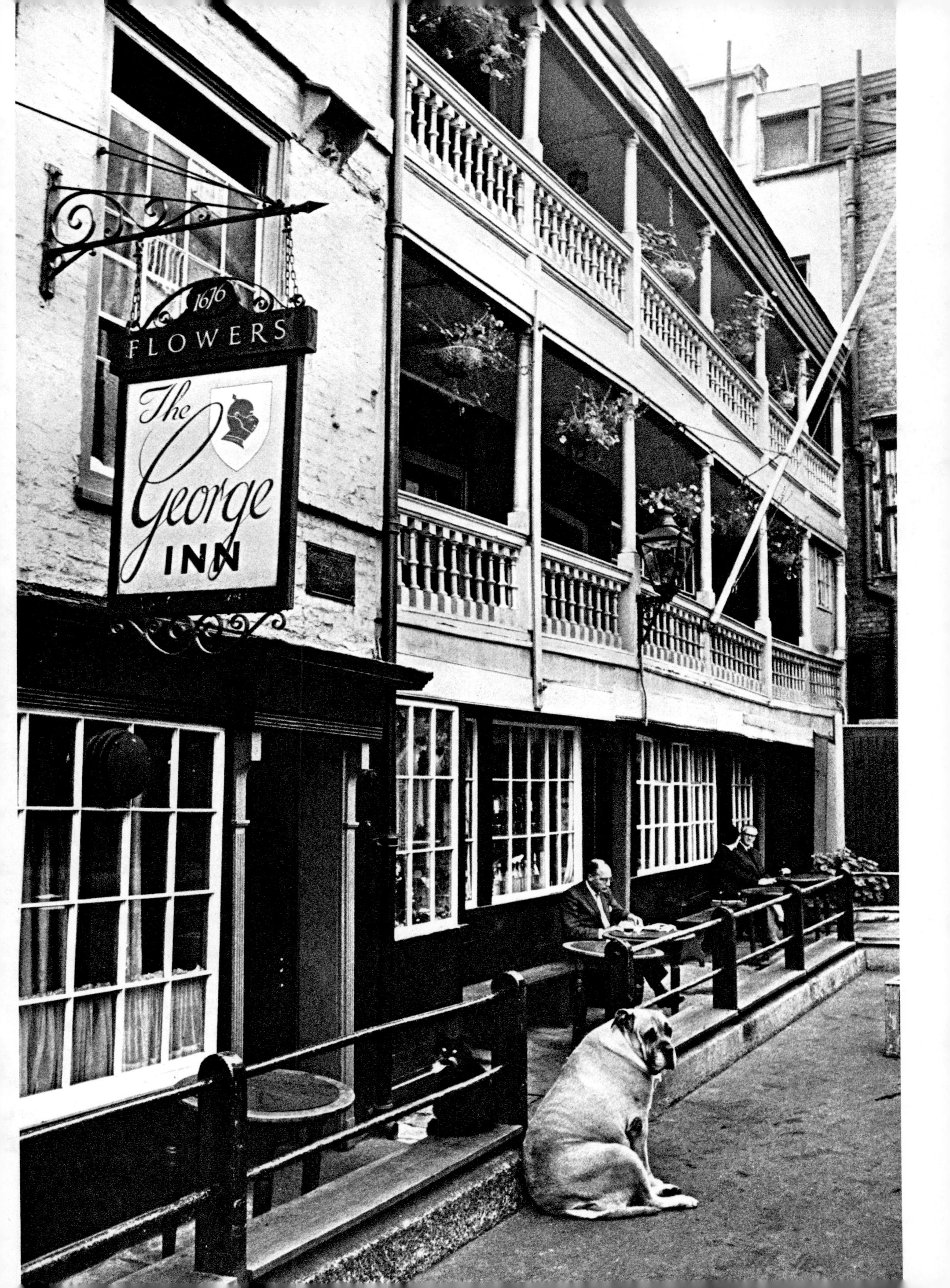
1676
FLOWERS
The George
INN

Dining room of the Ritz Hotel, Piccadilly; splendid decor nostalgic of a past age

Simpson's in the Strand; its reputation is based on the serving of best British meat

The Round Pond, Kensington Gardens

In the docks: high walls cut off the wharfs from the road

The Wellington Arch, Hyde Park Corner

Apsley House, home of the Duke of Wellington, now a museum

Decimus Burton's elegant screen, main entrance to Hyde Park

Admiralty Arch at the end of the Mall, part of a national memorial to Queen Victoria

Street corner betting shop, Notting Hill Gate. Revised gambling laws in 1960 made it possible for these shops to open and enabled anyone to bet on the afternoon's racing

Chelsea Pensioners and an aspect of London's fashion boom. Mary Quant's Bazaar boutique earned her an MBE and an international reputation

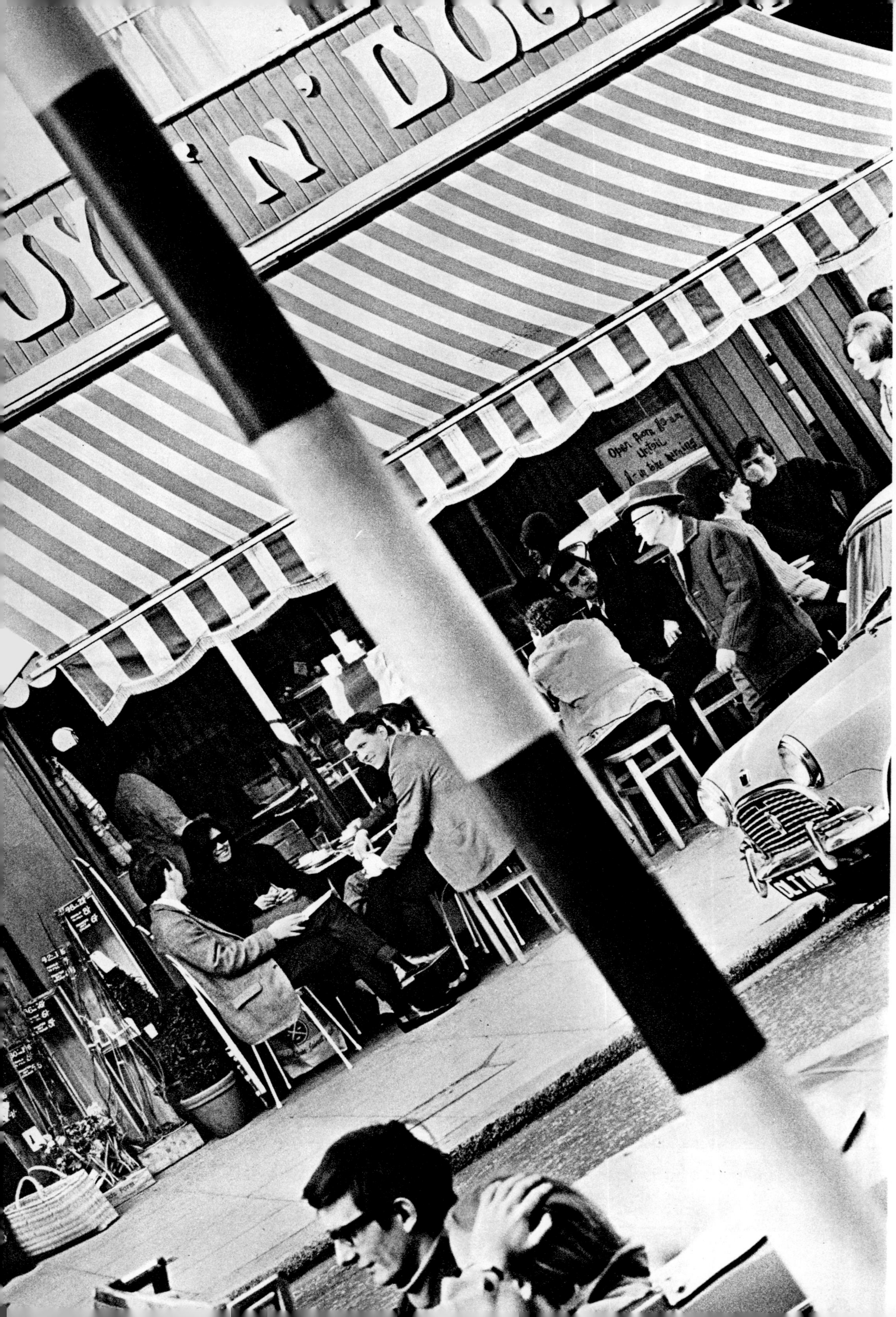

Underground Station; Notting Hill Gate

Left: King's Road, Chelsea; busy, varied street cutting through London's gayest, Bohemian quarter

Lincoln's Inn Fields, the largest square in London. Memorial seat

Right: St. James's Square. Possible to sleep in central London, in the sun, at midday

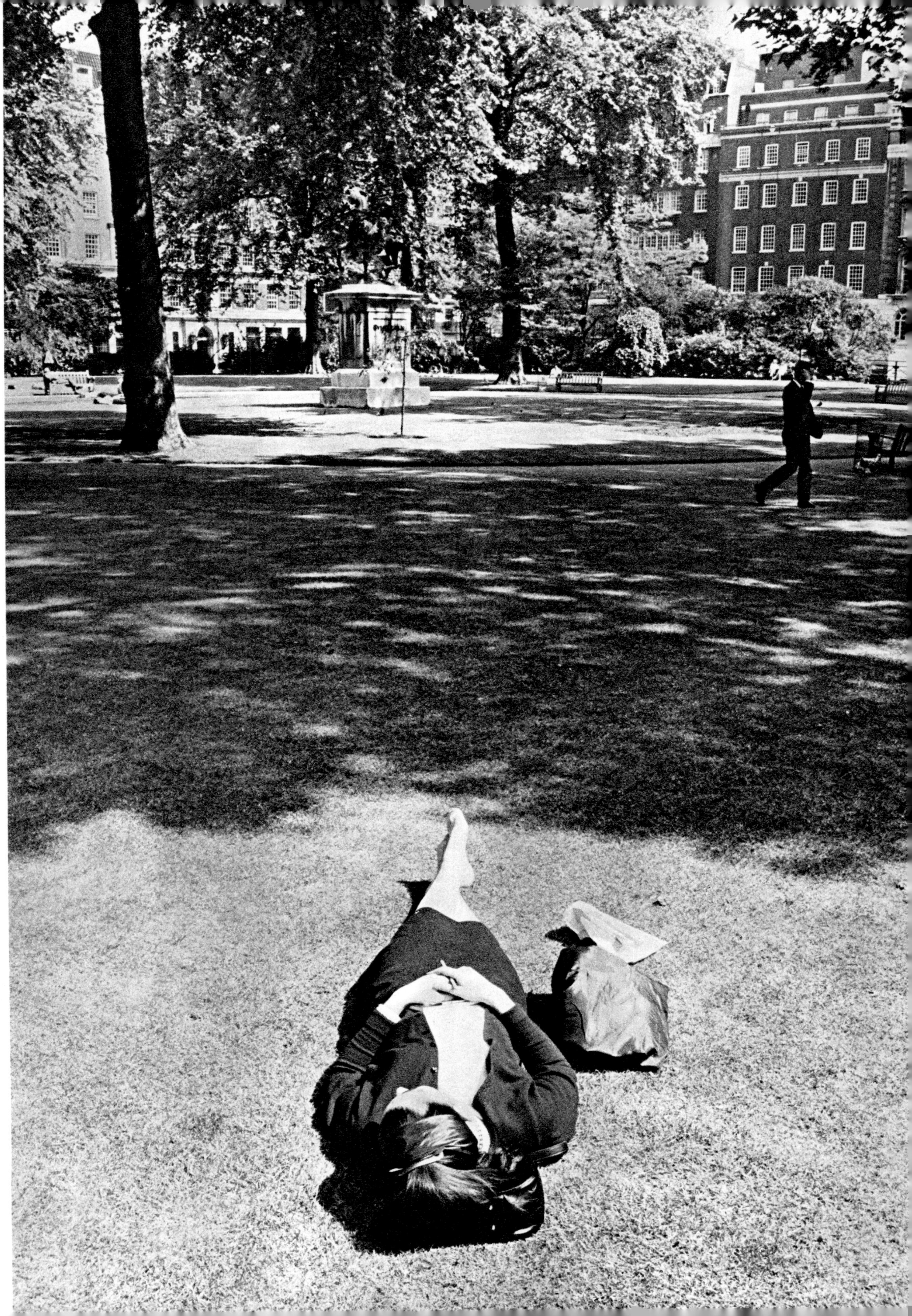

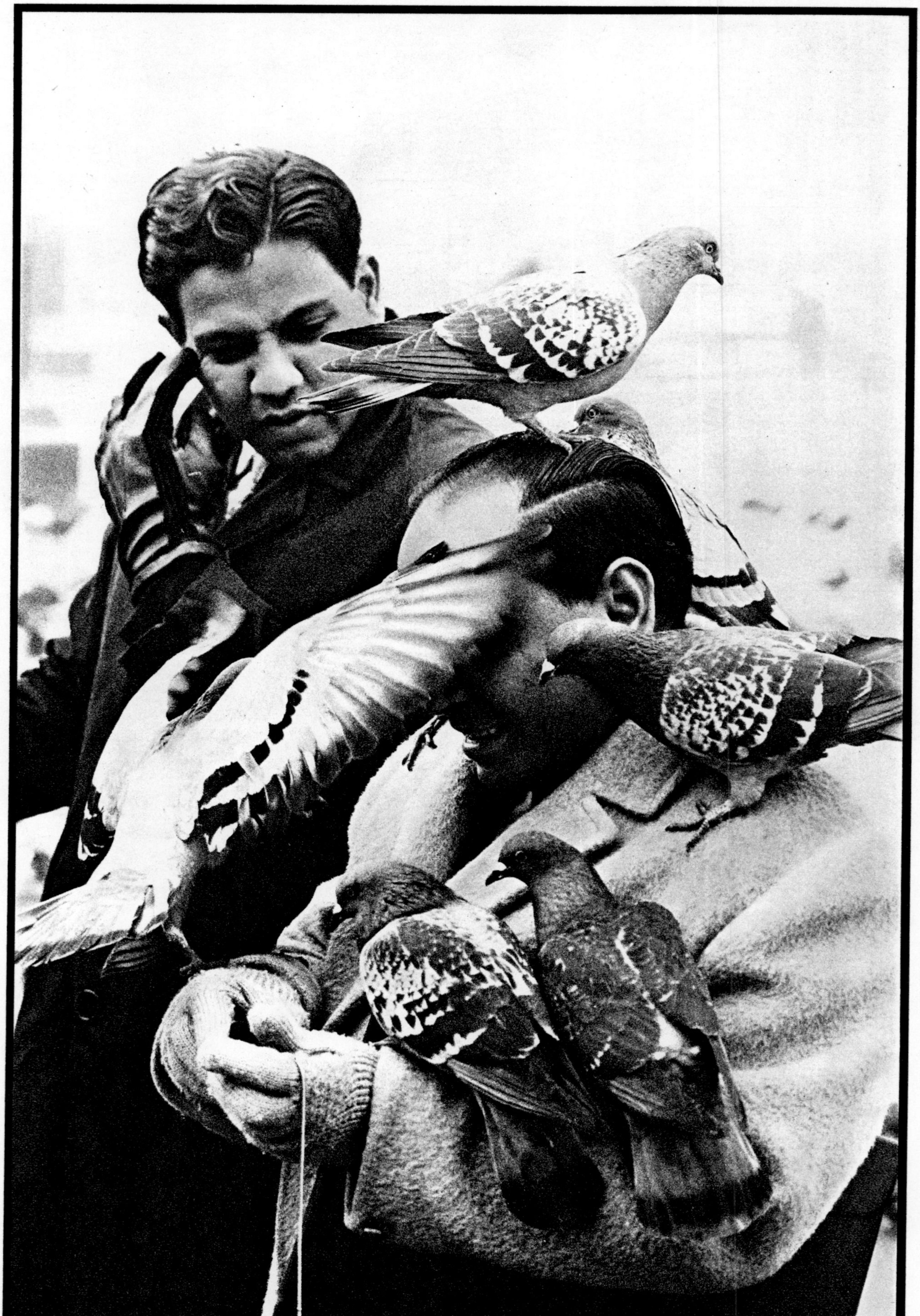

Trafalgar Square. The National Gallery and friendly pigeons

Lazing by the Thames at Richmond, a charming village-like suburb where the river becomes a tranquil, peaceful stream

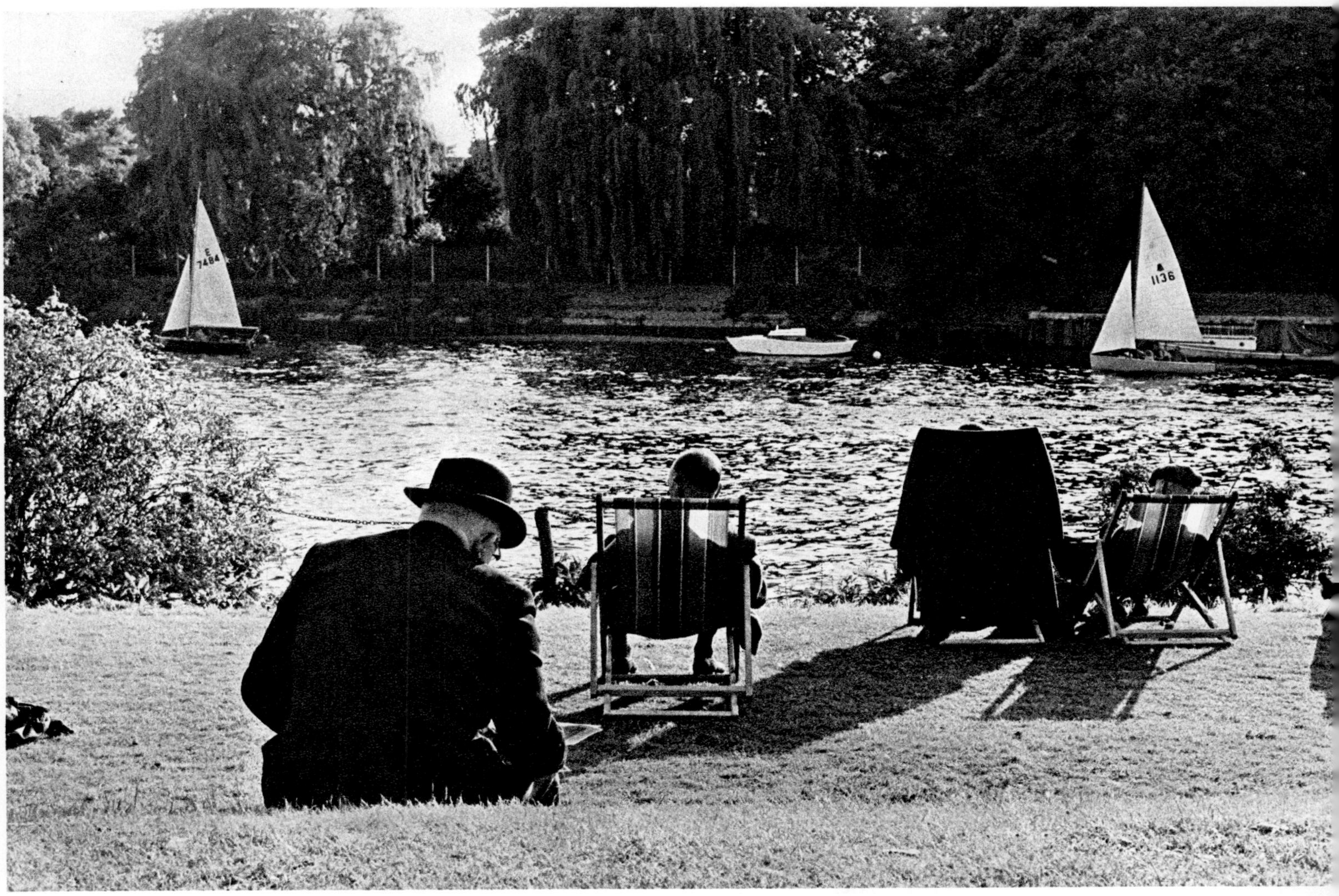
E
7484
1136

St. Paul's, Covent Garden. In the centre of theatreland, known as the actors' church. G. B. Shaw set the first scene of *Pygmalion* under its porch

Opposite top: feeding the pigeons in Trafalgar Square
Below: on duty outside the Horse Guards in Whitehall. Members of the Life Guards form part of the Household Cavalry

265

North Audley Street, from the roof of the Hilton Hotel

Little Venice: the barge Jason carries sightseers between here and Regent's Park Zoo

Lovers don't care: Richmond

Right: children and guy – an effigy of Guy Fawkes whose unsuccessful attempt to blow up parliament in 1605 is celebrated annually with fireworks

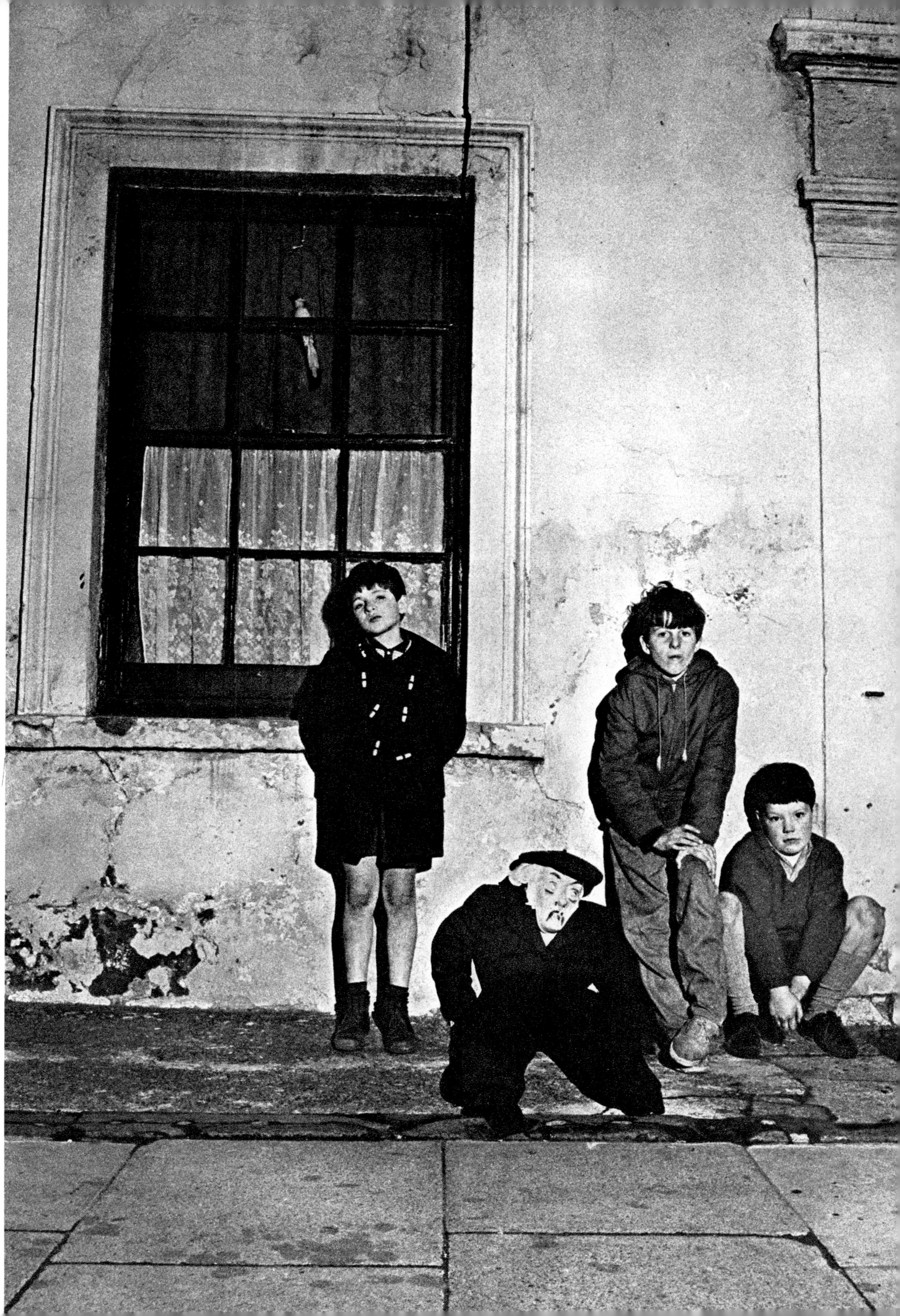

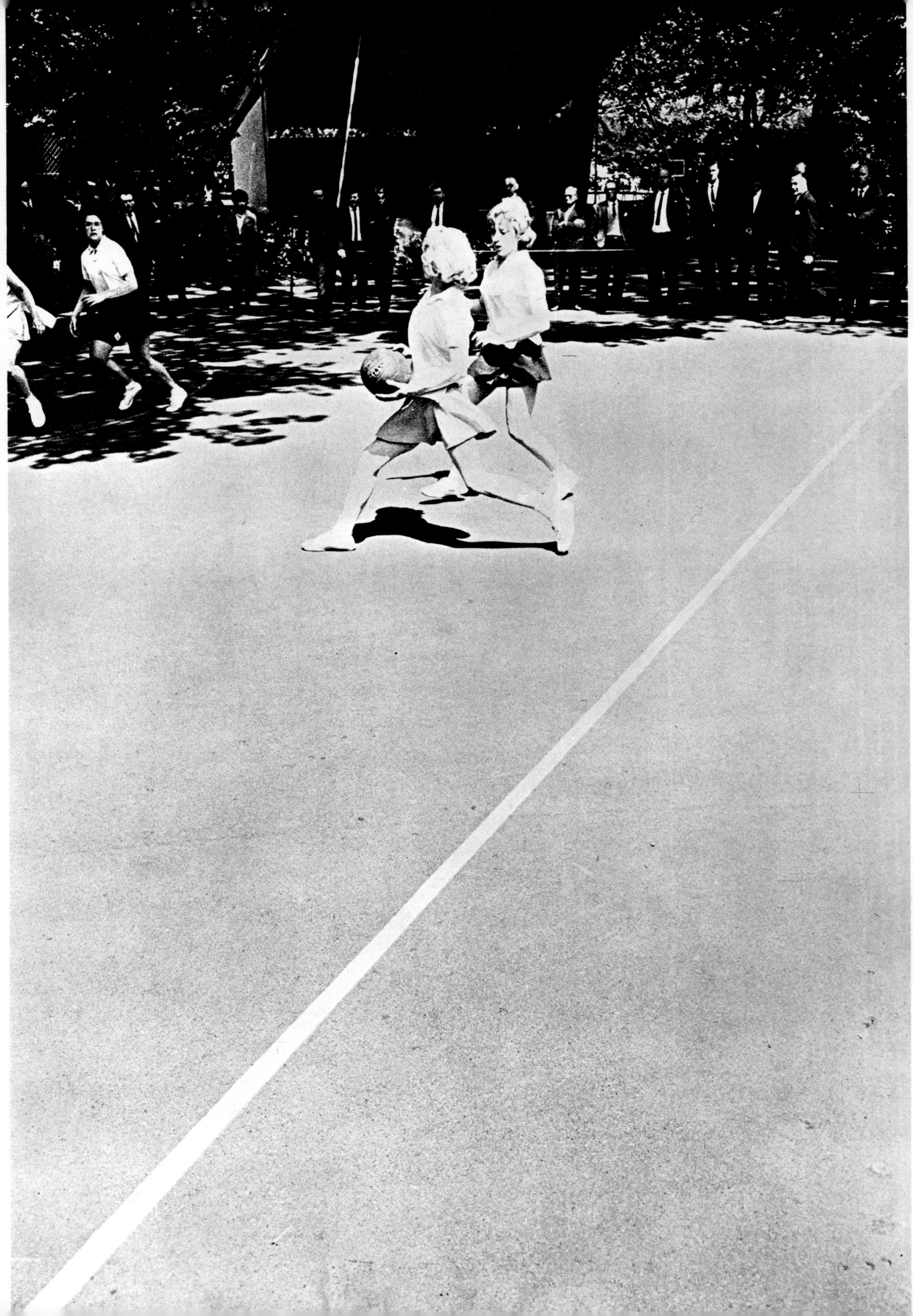

Sitting at ease, two Chelsea Pensioners in the grounds of the Chelsea Hospital, a home for old and disabled soldiers. *Left*: energy at lunchtime: netball in Lincoln's Inn fields

The Royal Horticultural Society's annual flower show in Chelsea. Also exhibited, fruit, vegetables, whole gardens

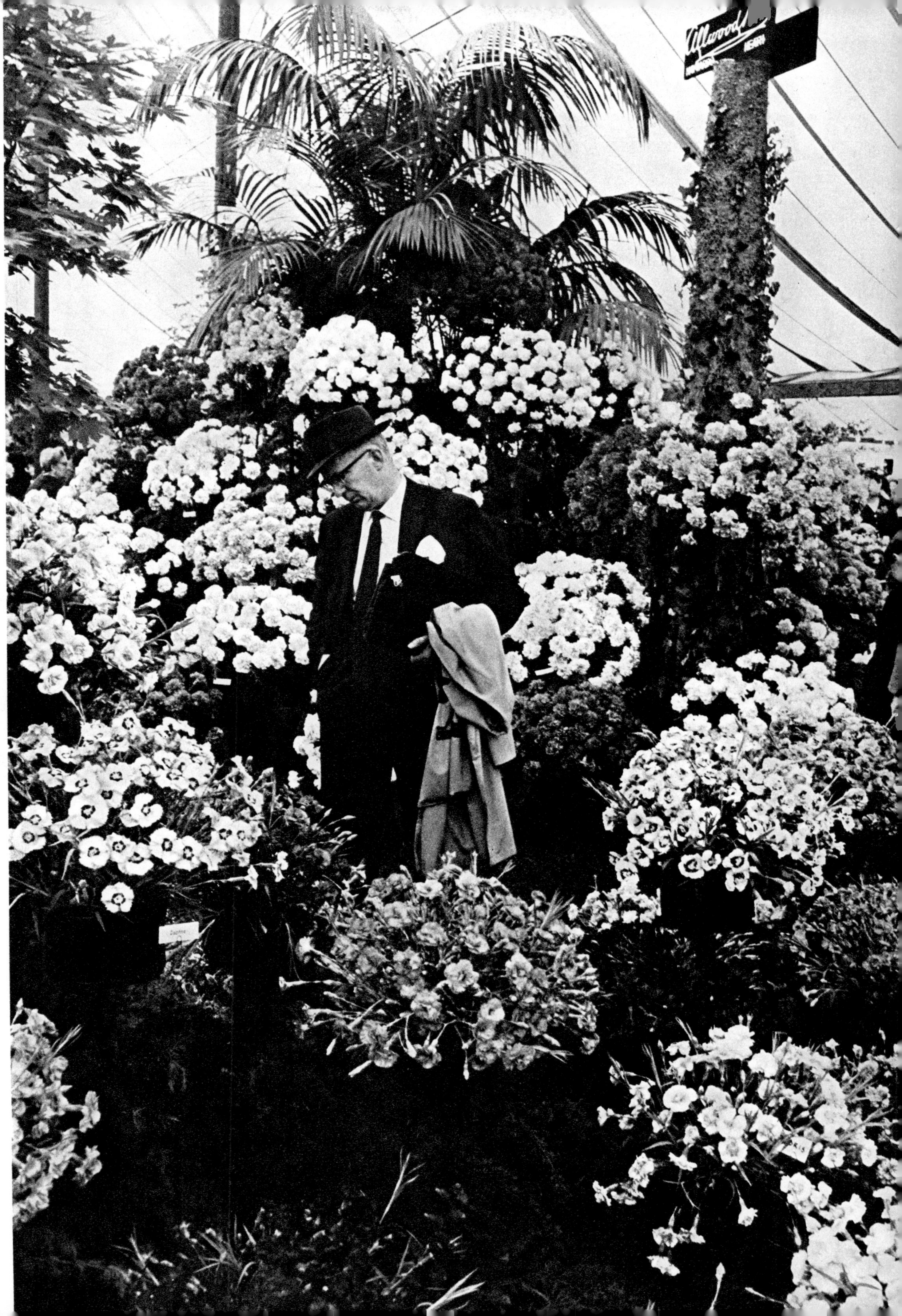

Bloomsbury Square; at 10 am, time to sit, read the newspapers, eat breakfast perhaps

Memorial statue to President Franklin D. Roosevelt, Grosvenor Square

Solitary lunch: Lincoln's Inn Fields

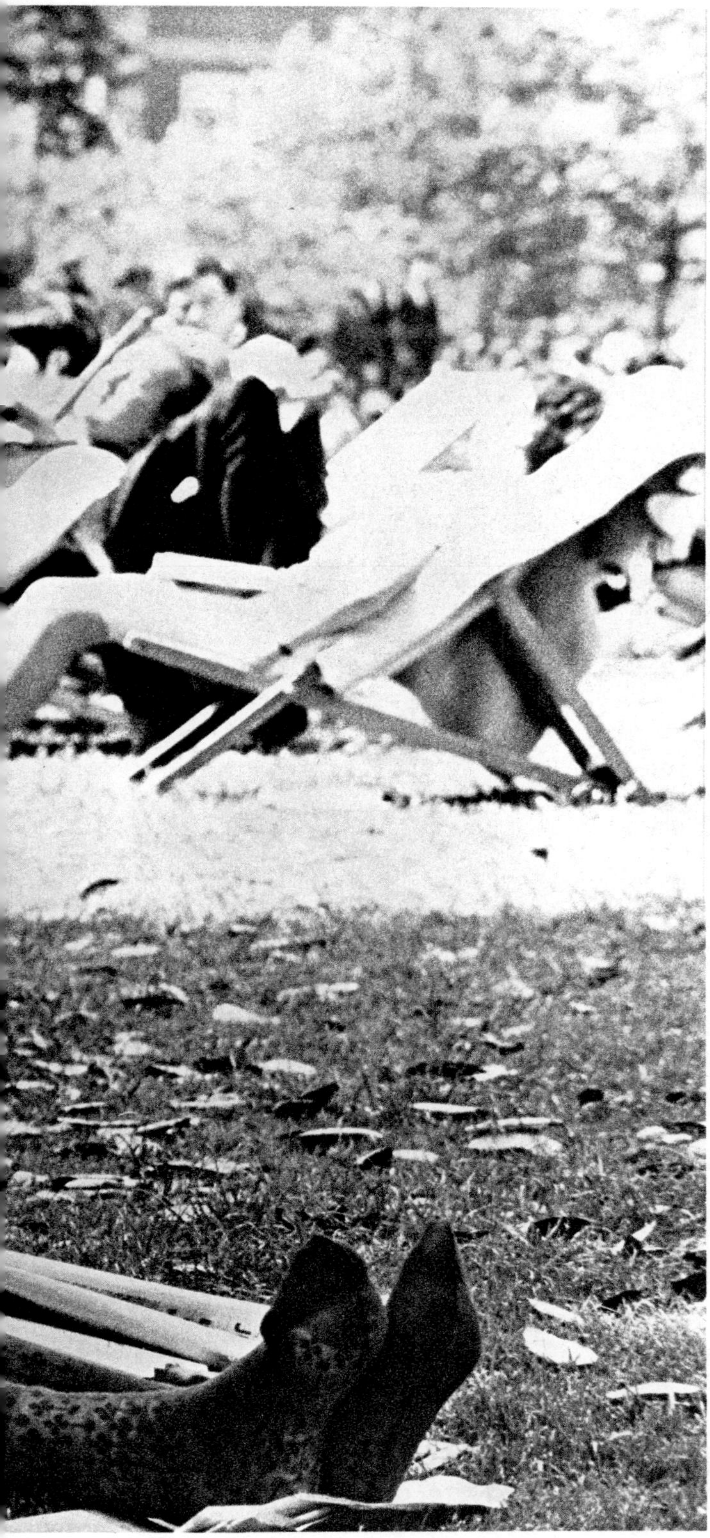

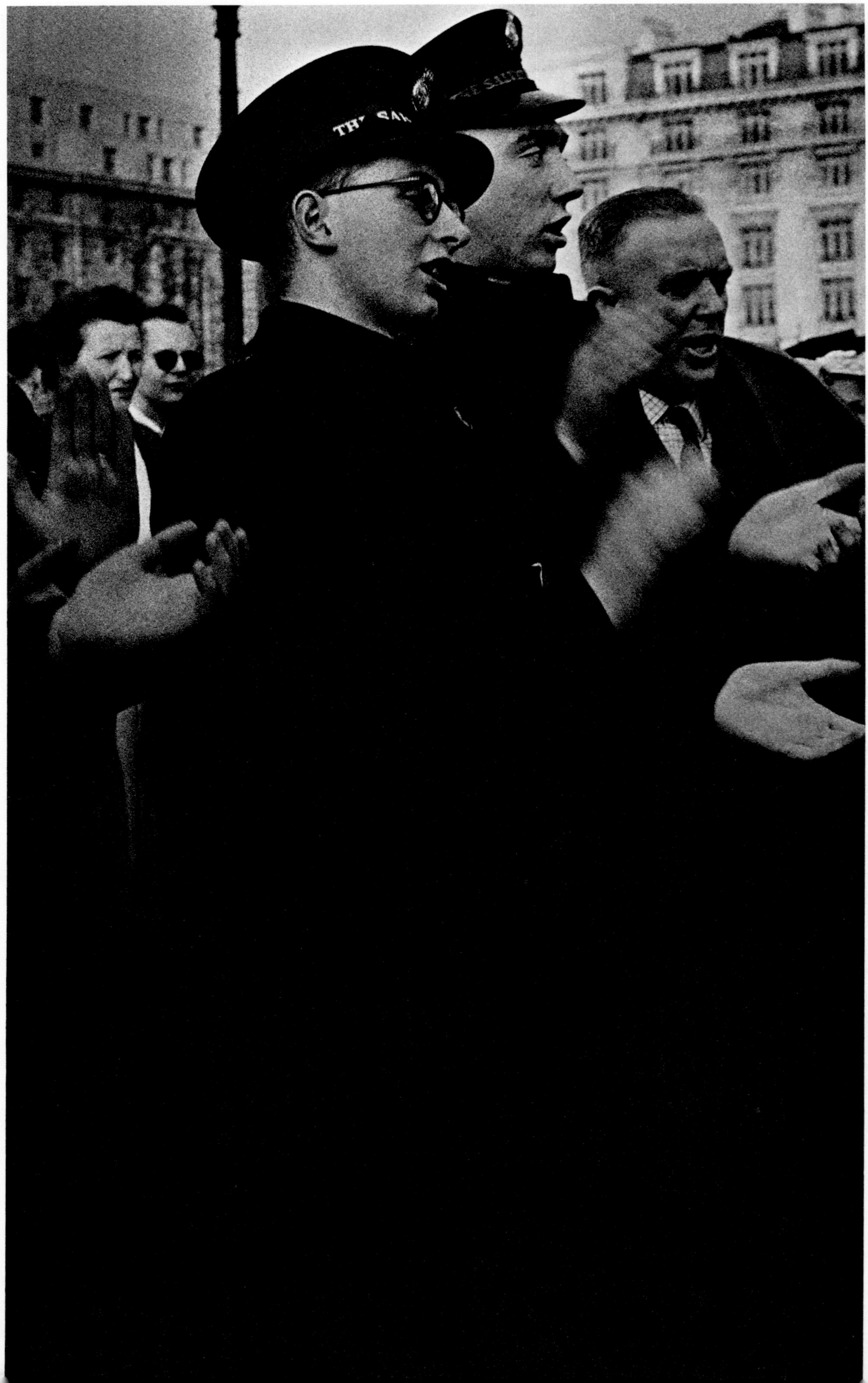

The Salvation Army Headquarters, Portobello Road, and (*left*) the Army in action at Speaker's Corner, Hyde Park

Sunset at Speaker's Corner, an area set off for anyone to address the crowds. Some listeners are attentive, others argumentative and some (*right*) indifferent

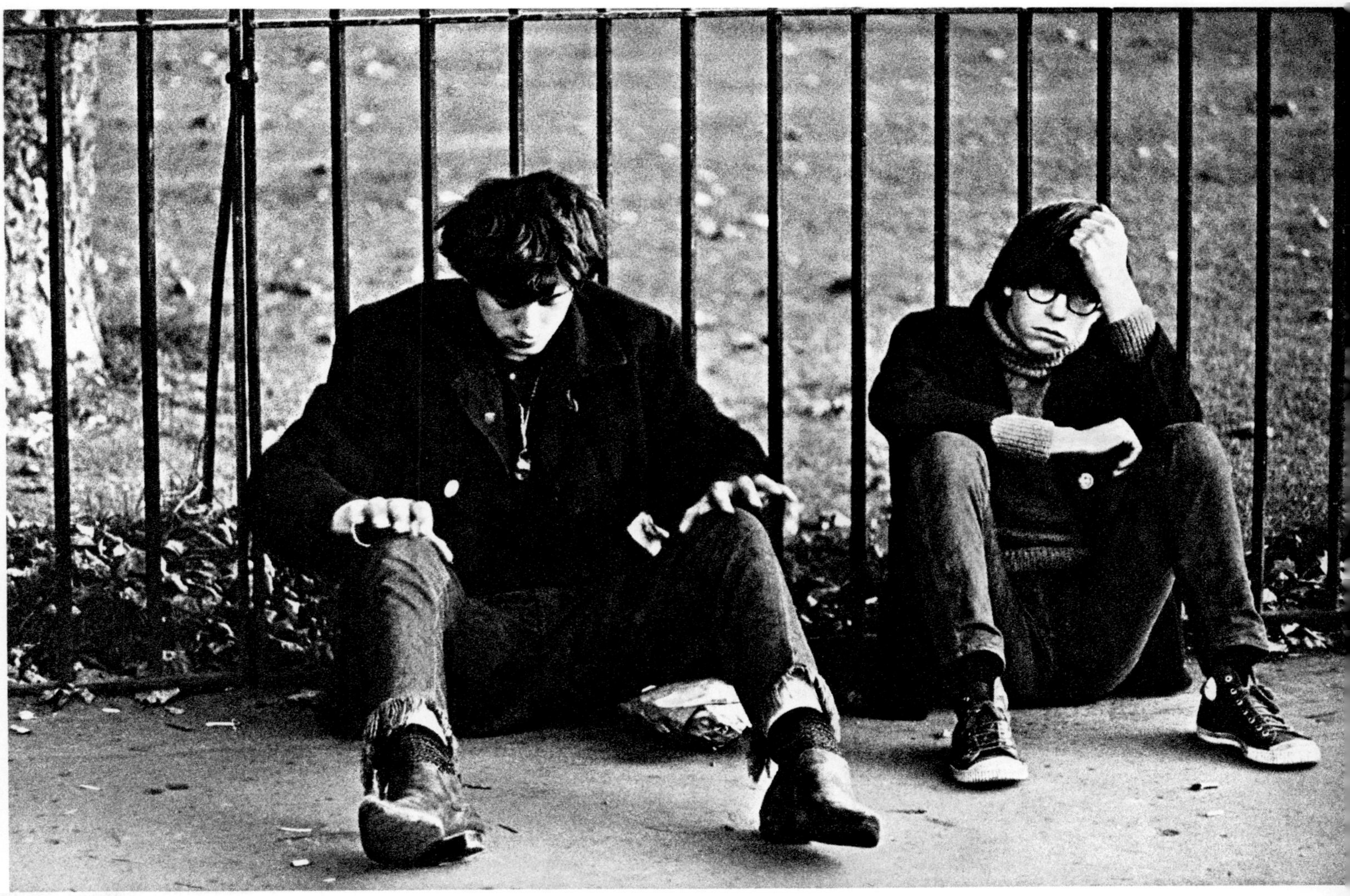

Highgate Cemetery: fine views and burial place of many distinguished people

"In loving and grateful memory of Colonel Francis Barker Montague late 4th (Queen's Own) Hussars, died November 9 1908." In Kensal Green Cemetery

Green Park, autumn. *Right:* sunset over the river at Hammersmith

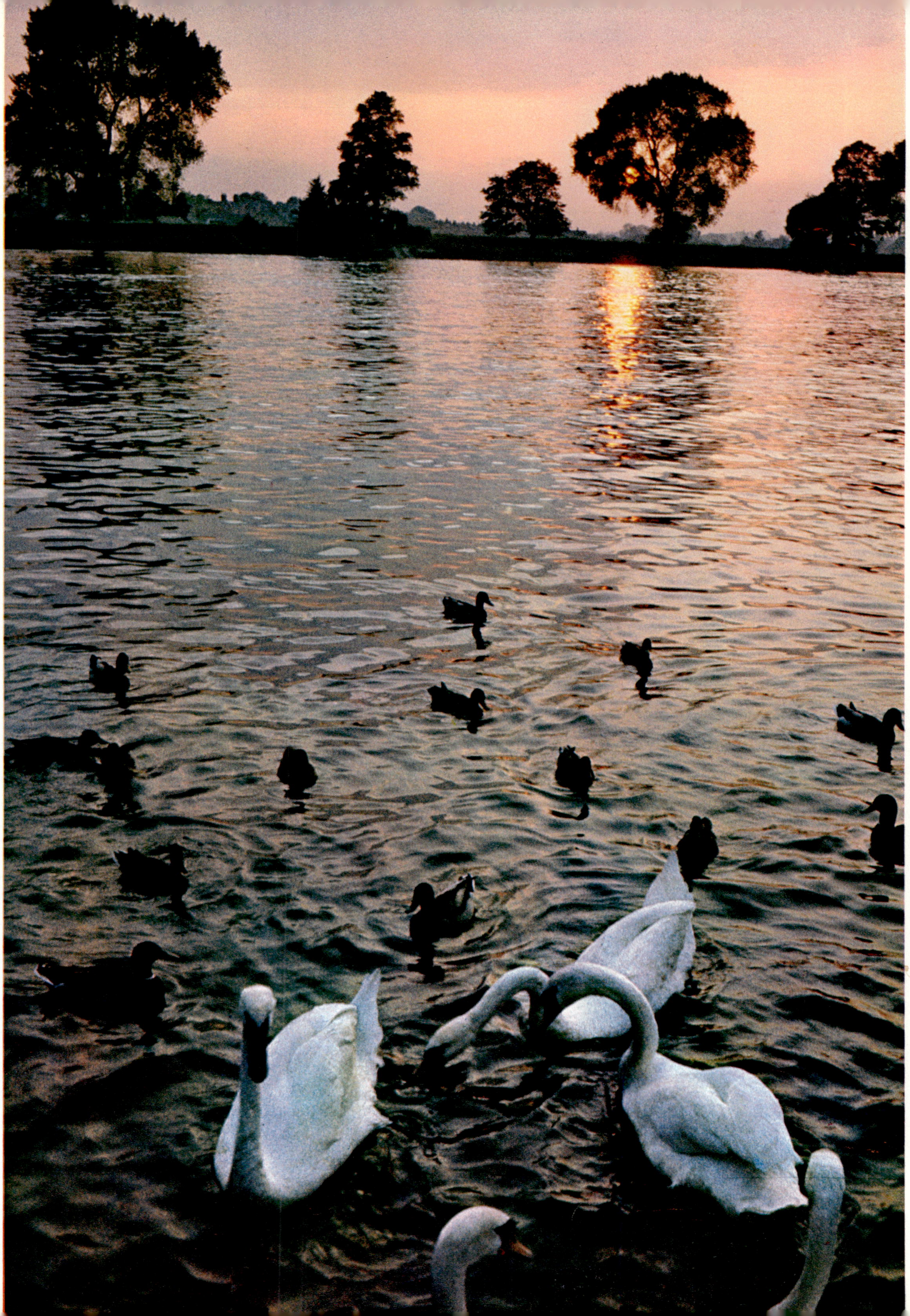

Piccadilly Circus: at night a dazzle of neon

Piccadilly Circus, with its statue of Eros in the centre

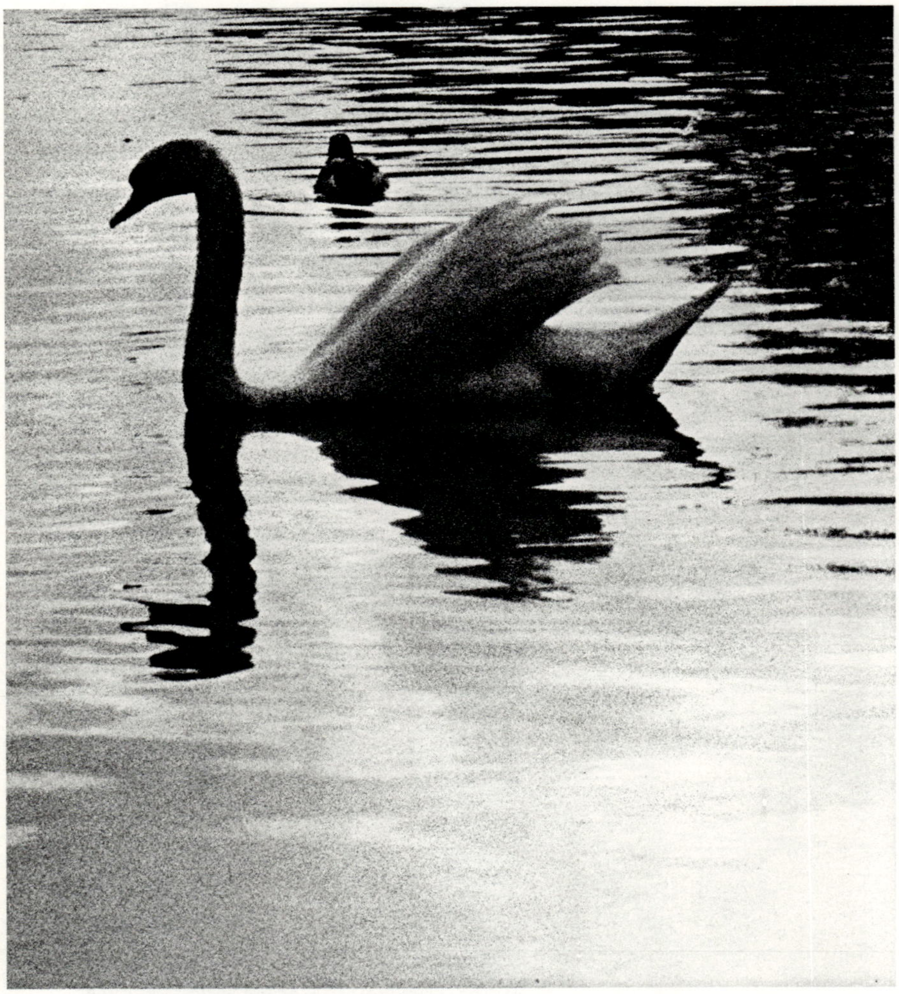

London Evening

As the sky dims and the neon flashes, London
makes its sumptuous appeal to the sensual
man. The town wears a new face, glittering
and enticing. During the summer,
light fine evenings indicate a tranquil time by
the river or just a stroll through the
easy streets. In winter thoughts turn to the theatre
or cinema. There are clubs to suit every taste
from teenage dancer to inveterate gambler;
there is the best theatre in the world and
it is the musical centre of the western world.
One may sing in a noisy, friendly pub
or spend time and care ordering a splendid meal
in one of the fine restaurants. London at
night makes its most dramatic appeal.

Sunset at Speakers' Corner, near Marble Arch, a space reserved for those with something to get off their chests

The lights go on in Trafalgar Square

Opposite: Buskers entertain cinema queues in Leicester Square

McQUEEN
G. ROBINSON
MARGRET
THE
MECCA
DANCING
TWICE - A - DAY
McQUEEN • ROBINSON • MARGRET
CINCINNATI KID
DANCING

A girl, a boy, a guitar: wandering home on a summer evening across Primrose Hill

Opposite: Recital: at the Wigmore Hall where a solo artist usually makes his London debut

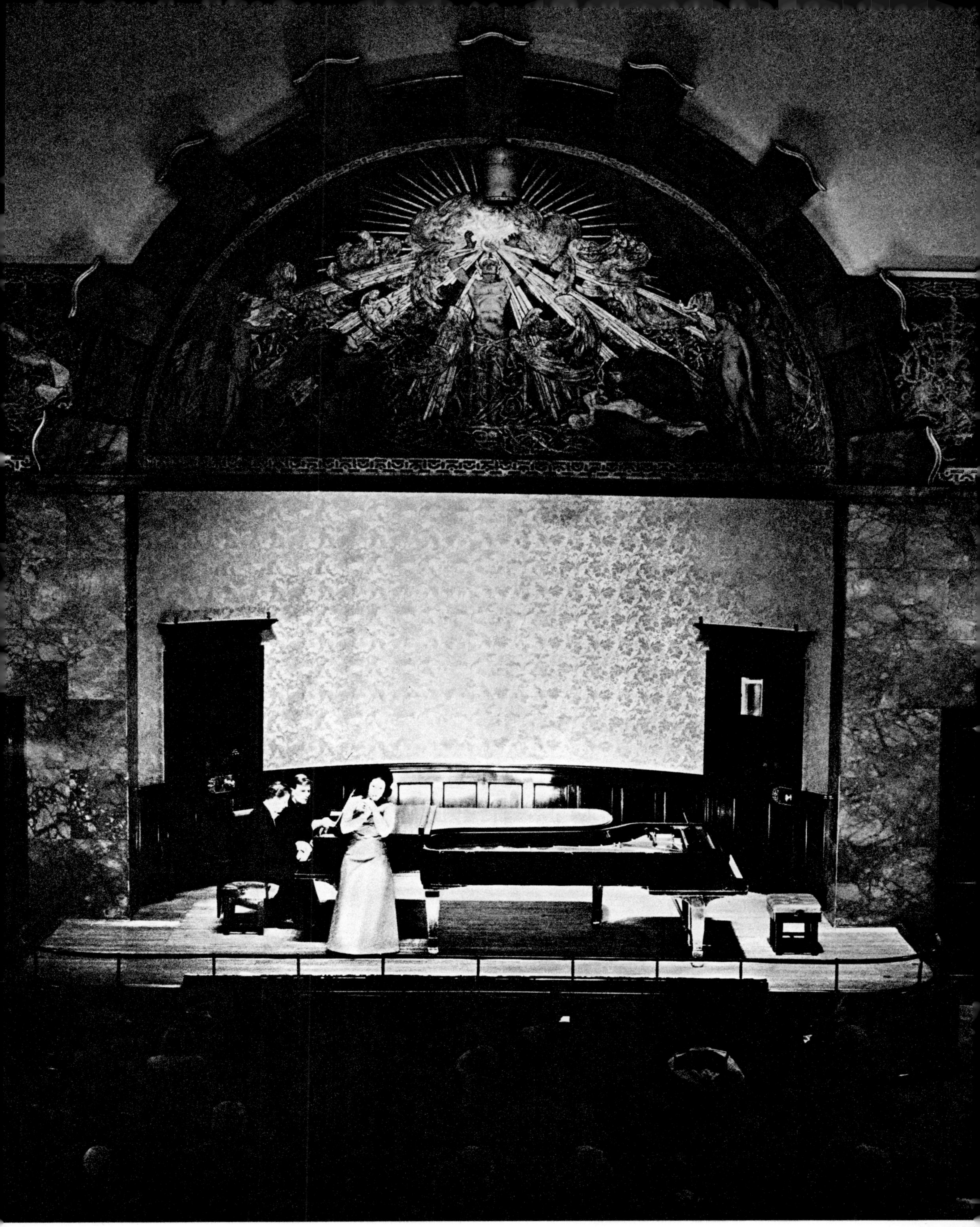

Music: the patriotic outburst of the last night of the Henry Wood Promenade Concerts at the Albert Hall. Sir Malcolm Sargent conducts the audience, Josephine Veasey is the soloist, in *Rule Britannia*

Opposite: the River Thames rises at full tide onto the street in Chiswick Mall

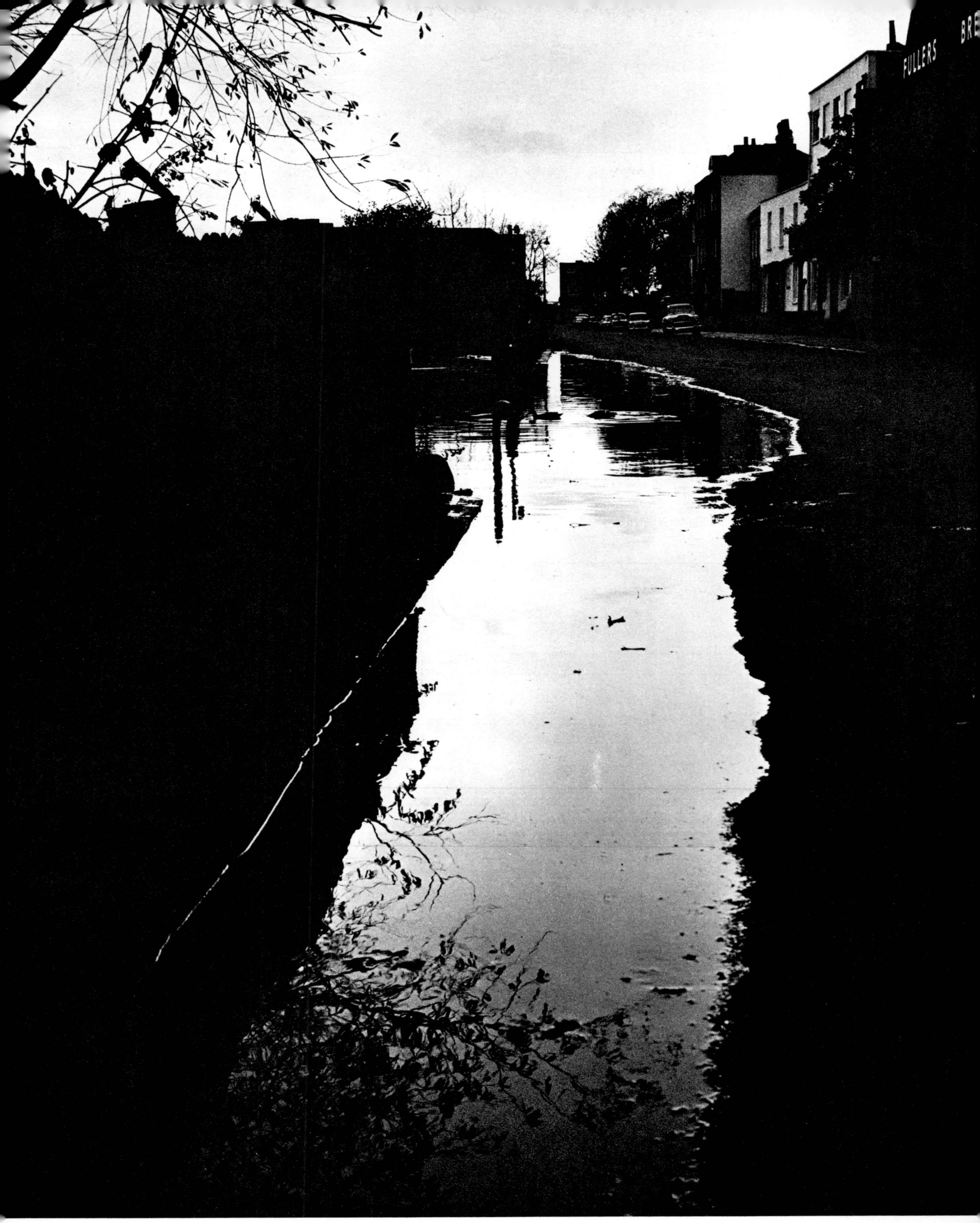
FULLERS

First night: the audience arrives at the Garrick Theatre. The celebrated actor's portrait hangs over the foyer bar

IMMEDIATE SERVICE
AT THE INTERVAL
PLEASE PLACE YOUR
ORDER NOW

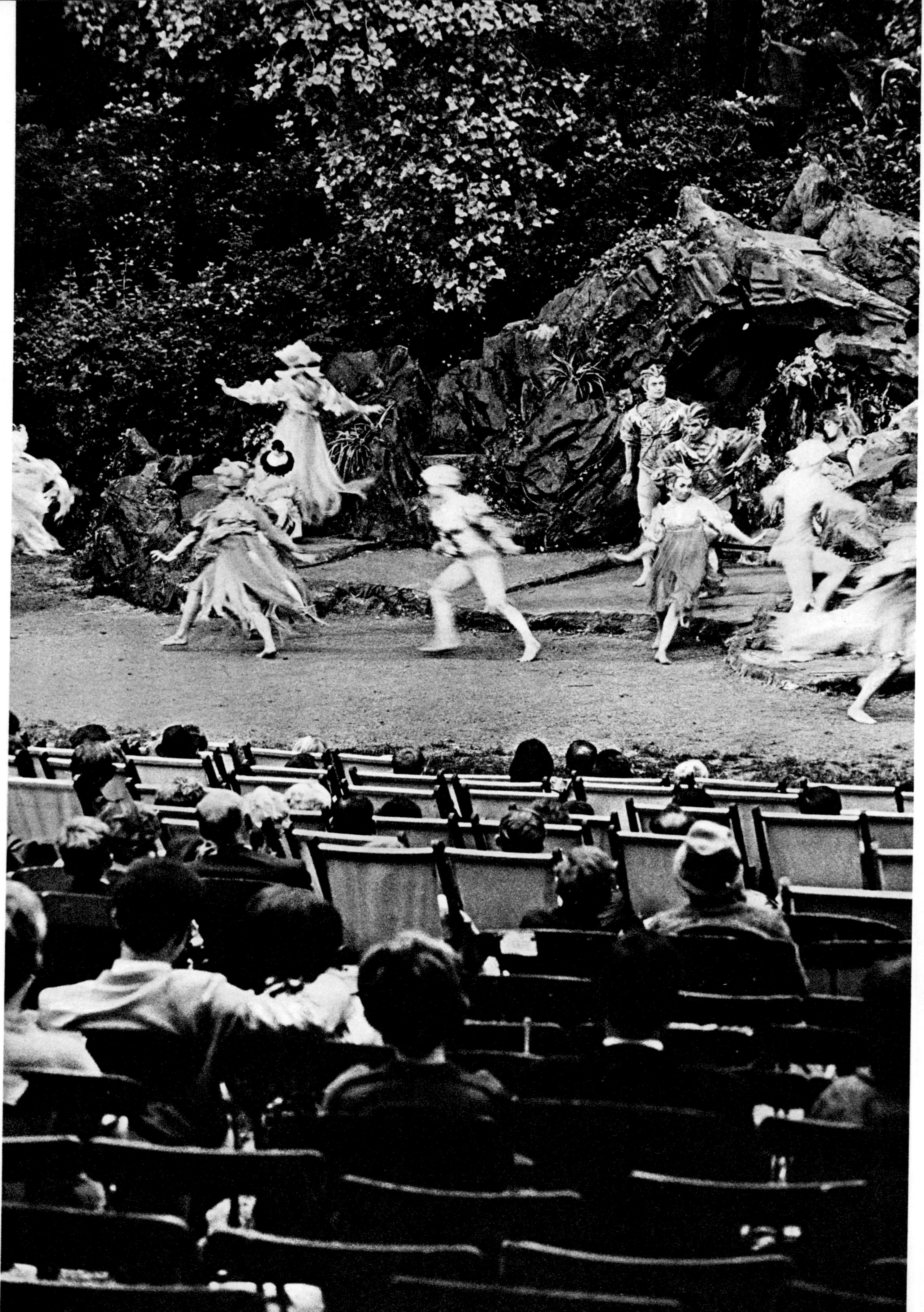

Smoke-filled room: Miss Blossom Dearie plays the piano and sings at Ronnie Scott's Club

Fresh air: in Regent's Park open-air theatre, performances of Shakespeare are an annual event. Here, *A Midsummer Night's Dream*

Dame Margot Fonteyn and Rudolf Nureyev take their calls before the monogrammed curtain of the Royal Opera House after a performance of *Giselle*

Evening out: floorshow at the Pigalle theatre-restaurant in Piccadilly

Evening out: the crush bar at the Royal Opera House, Covent Garden

At Ronnie Scott's club, alto-sax Lee Konitz plays. This is London's only jazz club – though others come and go – and Scott engages the best soloists from both sides of the Atlantic

East End: Tubby Isaacs' fish stall, near Aldgate East underground station where late-night revellers will pause for cockles, mussels, whelks and prawns

West End: night-time window-shopping in the Burlington Arcade

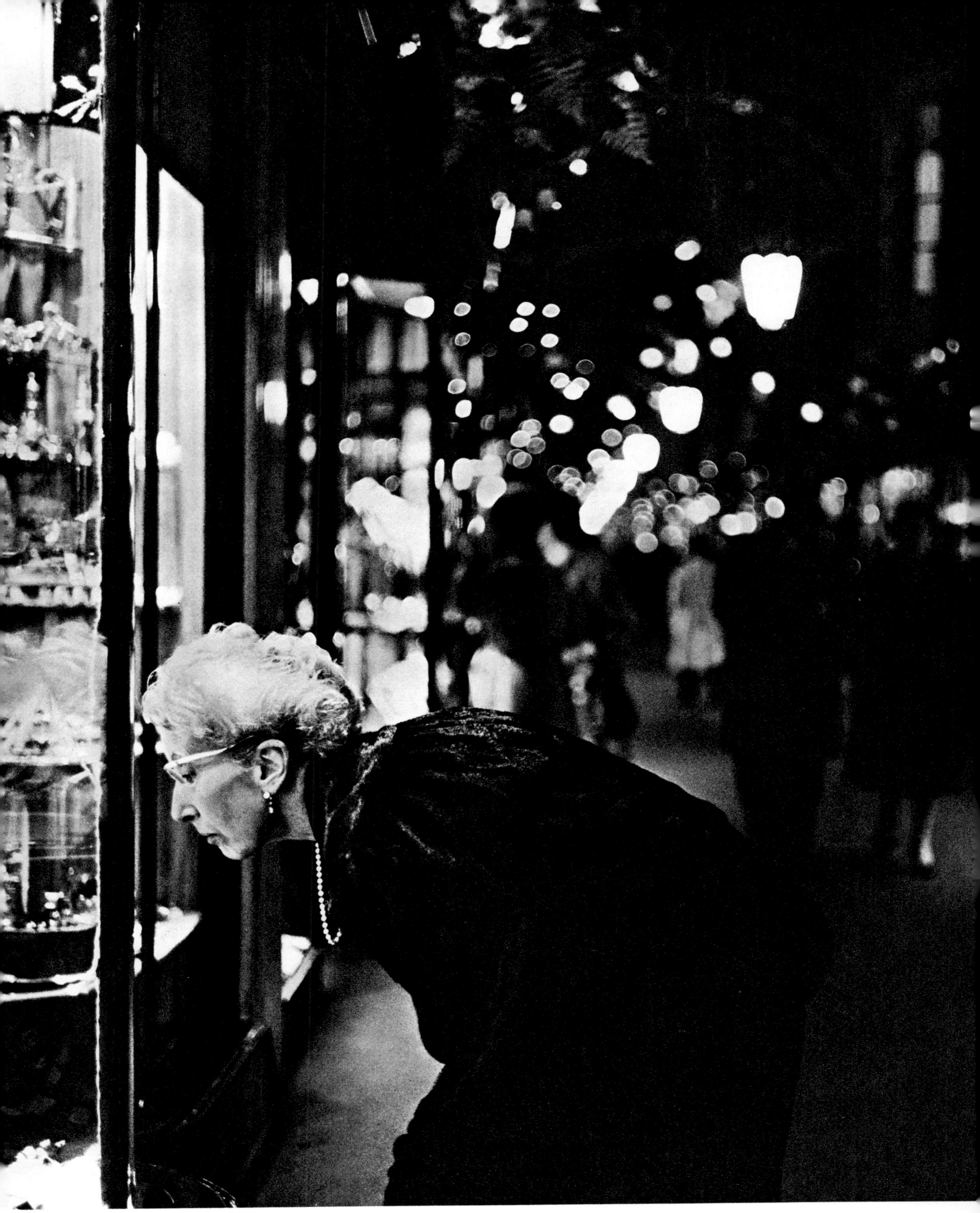

Shop windows on Oxford Street, enticement for evening strollers

Dinner in the Edwardian splendour of Rule's in Maiden Lane where traditional English food is a speciality

Kaleriya Fedicheva, ballerina of The Leningrad State Kirov Ballet rehearses for the opening performance of *Swan Lake* when the company visited the Royal Opera House, Covent Garden. Foreign ballet companies are regular visitors

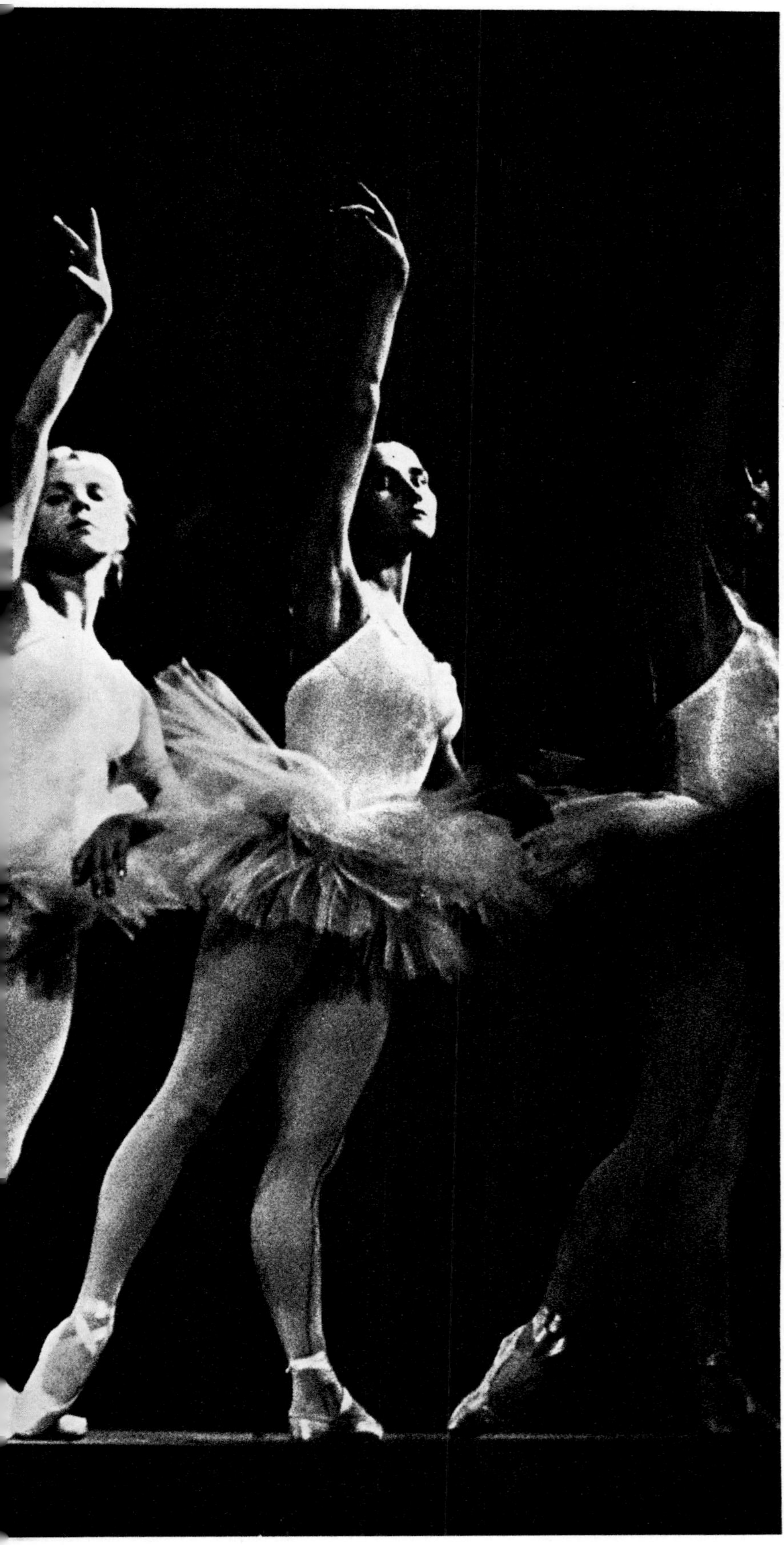

The Palm Beach Club in Berkeley Street, one of London's elegant gaming clubs

Outside an Oxford Street Club called Tiles that caters for young people, offers beat groups and dancing

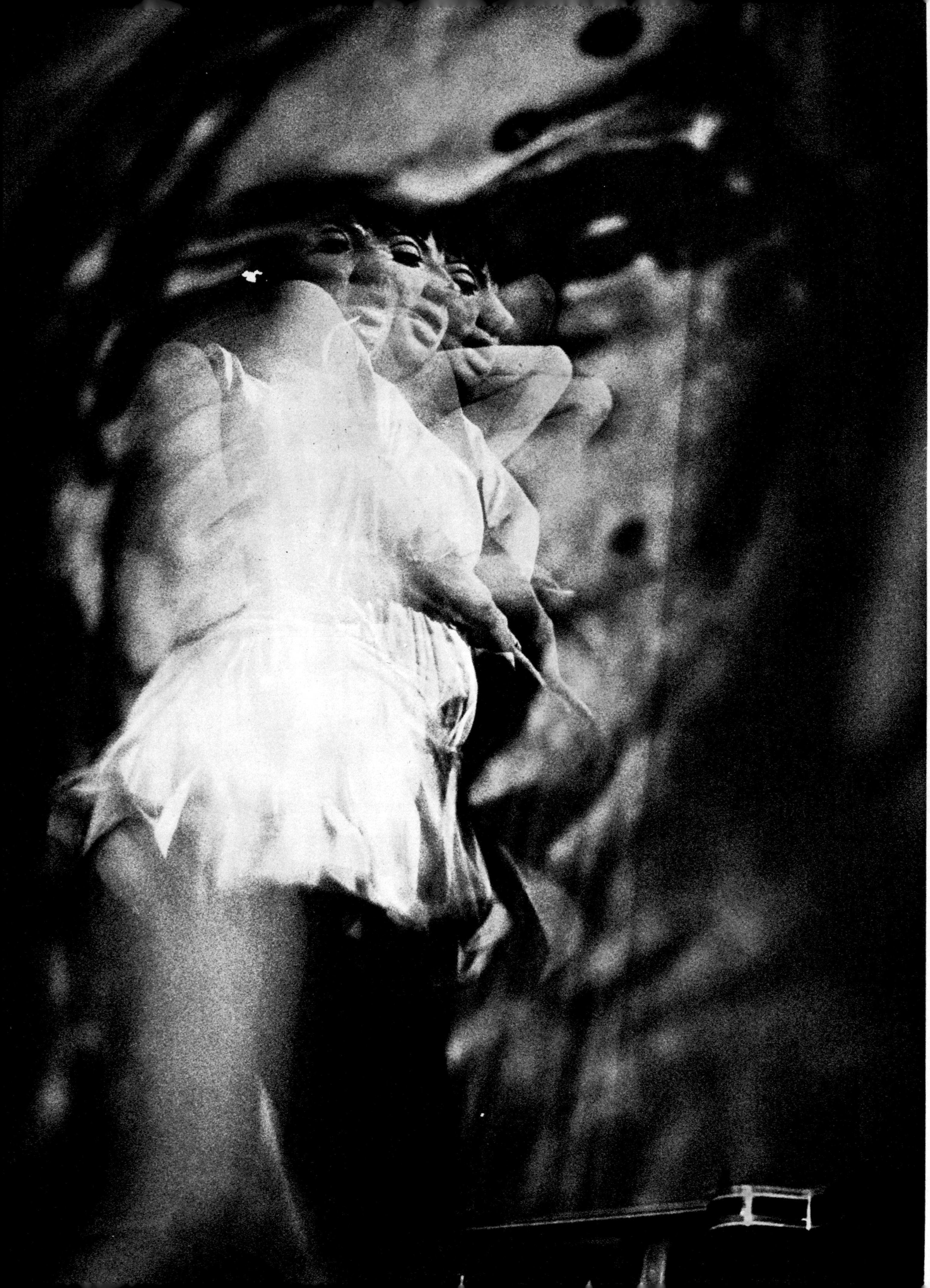

Contrasting aspects of night life: female impersonator Danny la Rue at his own club in Hanover Square, and (*left*) dancing at the Round House where improvised, uninhibited events take place

Pub-life flourishes in the East End. Local lads drink and watch as Kim Cordell sings at the Watermans Arms in the Isle of Dogs – an area formed by a loop in the Thames and the docks

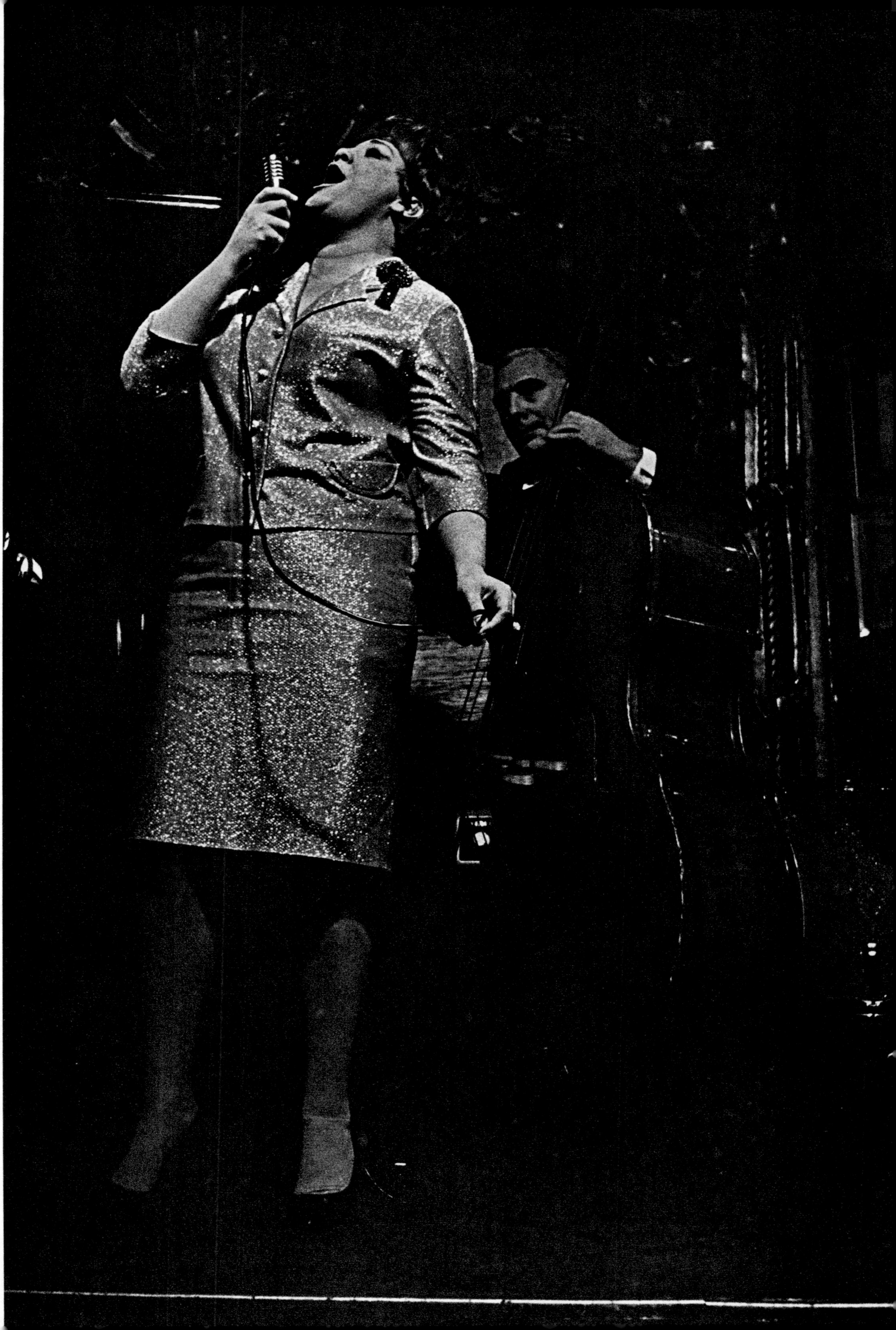

End of a long day: the moon rides high over a house in Wimbledon. But already across the city the markets are full of activity preparing for another day . . .

KILLYMOON

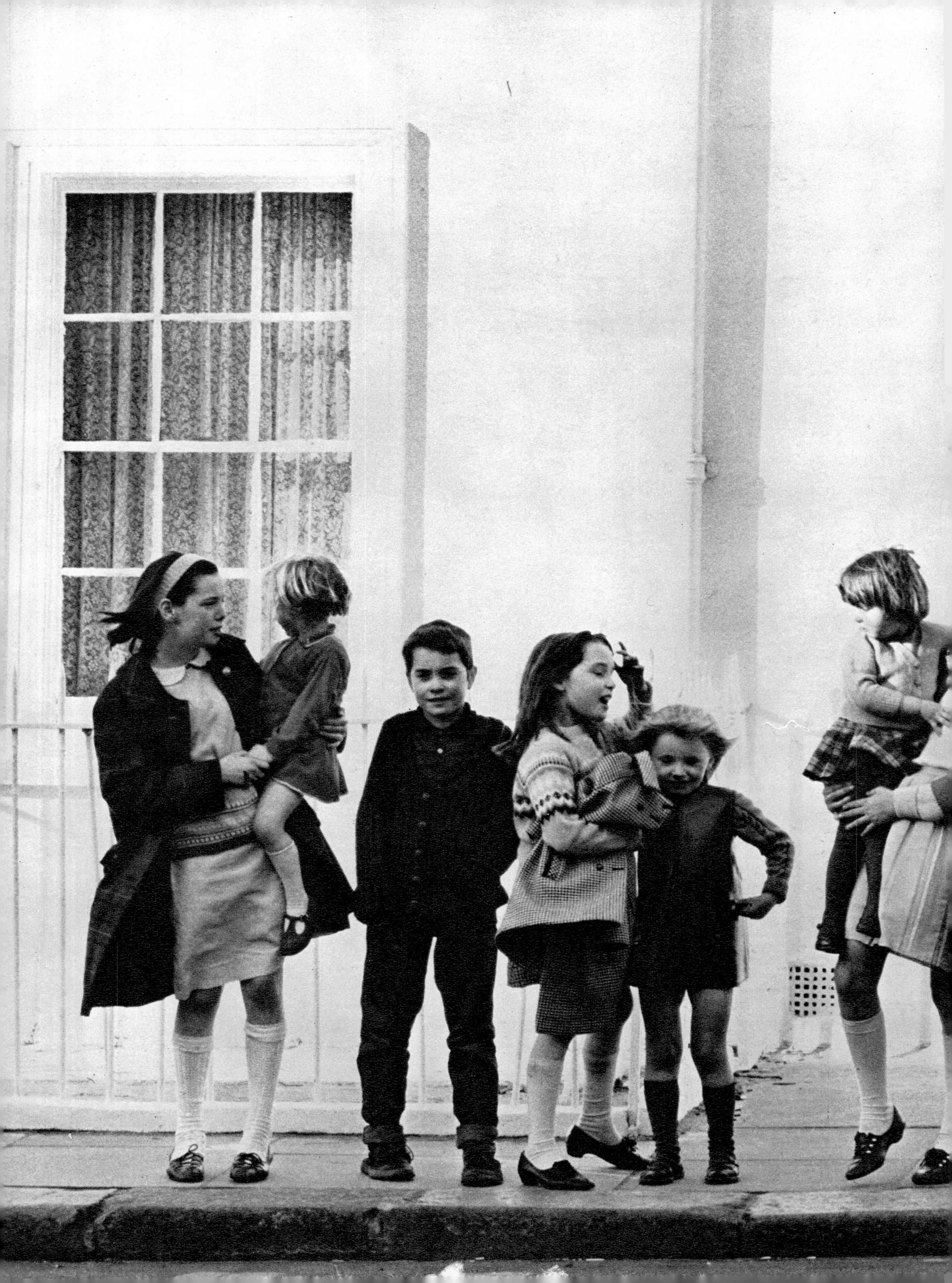